MISSION ACCOMPLISHED:
A Perfect Season

THE NEWSPAPER NETWORK OF CENTRAL OHIO PRESENTS THE HISTORY-MAKING SEASON OF THE OHIO STATE UNIVERSITY BUCKEYES

A result of the hard work of all the newspaper staffs of NNCO.

Compiled by Jason Maddux,
Coordinating and Online Editor, Newspaper Network of Central Ohio

n
newspaper network
OF CENTRAL OHIO

A GANNETT GROUP

www.centralohio.com

Acknowledgments

Mission Accomplished: A Perfect Season
Newspaper Network of Central Ohio

Nickolas F. Monico
President

Executive in Charge of Project
Alfred J. Getler
Vice President/Marketing and Circulation

Project Editor
Jason Maddux
Group Coordinating Editor/Online Editor

Tom Brennan
Group Senior Editor

THE PHOTOGRAPHERS

William P. Cannon
Lancaster Eagle-Gazette

Christopher Crook
Zanesville Times Recorder

Ben French
Fremont News-Messenger

Kevin Graff
Newark Advocate

Jeff Groves
Newark Advocate

Trevor Jones
Coshocton Tribune

Daniel Melograna
Mansfield News Journal

James Miller
Marion Star

Jason J. Molyet
Mansfield News Journal

Dave Polcyn
Mansfield News Journal

Bill Sinden
Marion Star

Dante Smith
Zanesville Times Recorder

Copyright© 2003 • ISBN: 1-932129-35-9

TABLE OF CONTENTS

Introduction

It was worth the wait.

It took 16 years of reporting on the Ohio State Buckeyes — chronicling all home and away games — for me to arrive at a national championship.

If I'm never part of college football nirvana again, I always will be able to relive the memories of that spellbinding 31-24 double-overtime victory over Miami in the Fiesta Bowl as if they happened yesterday.

I'm sure you feel the same.

Perhaps more than the title game itself, I'll remember the improbable events leading up to that almost surreal night in the desert — the fourth-and-one touchdown pass to

Jon Spencer

Michael Jenkins to beat Purdue; the overtime escape at Illinois the following week; and Will Allen's goal-line interception on the final play against bitter rival Michigan the week after that.

It was a perfect season of brilliant halftime adjustments, second-half comebacks, fourth-quarter rallies and breathtaking flirtations with defeat.

For someone who finds amusement parks downright scary, it was the kind of wild ride I usually avoid.

But if you want to strap me in again in 2003, I'd love another front row seat.

Jon Spencer, a sports reporter for the Mansfield News Journal, has covered Ohio State since 1987, Earle Bruce's last year as coach. He is the Ohio State football beat reporter for the Newspaper Network of Central Ohio.

"This is for coach Tressel: A year ago, we sat in a room and we had a mission. Coach, mission accomplished. Go Bucks."

— OSU strong safety Mike Doss, during the national championship celebration at Ohio Stadium on Jan. 18, 2003.

Foreword

By Rex Kern with Jay Hansen

National championships often are viewed as individual accomplishments achieved by great individual players. In truth, there is nothing individual about any national championship — not the one the 1968 Buckeyes won, nor the one that the 2002 team claimed. Individuals don't win championships. Teams do — and winning teams aren't formed in a single season.

Jim Tressel started building toward a championship the first day he walked on to the practice fields at the Woody Hayes Athletic Center. I was there that day, and there was

Rex Kern

nothing incredibly glamorous to be seen … nothing that would outwardly suggest greatness. But greatness can be found in simplicity, and that day Jim was emphasizing the simple things — the nuts-and-bolts basics of football.

This approach struck me. In my playing days, Woody Hayes was a stickler for detail. When I talked to Jim after that practice, I heard a similar theme. Jim said the team was going back to the basics; these Buckeyes were going to learn from the ground up, much like Woody's Ohio State teams did. I firmly believe a national championship was hatched that day. The little things Jim started working on built on one another and became big things. They were building blocks for success. What we saw in Tempe on Jan. 3 was a product of the foundational work Jim was accentuating from day one.

Equally important has been Jim's emphasis on the team as a family. The synergy of this squad was an important unseen element that played a major role in our success. That's probably why so many people favored Miami — a team with great measurable talent and speed. You can't measure cohesiveness or heart, so it's easy to overlook. But those intangibles are important strengths we developed throughout the season. Our positive attitude helped us through tough times, and I think Jim fostered that demeanor. He helped a group of guys learn to care for one another and work together as a team. The guys on the 1968 championship team had a genuine affection for each other, and I think this squad had a similar bond.

How did Jim accomplish this? In many ways, I'm sure. But you can't overlook how he embraced Ohio State's storied football tradition. When he took over as coach, Jim asked former Ohio State players to write a letter explaining what being a Buckeye meant to them in their lives. Those letters are posted in the locker room, and kids can read them and see what Ohio State meant to a Paul Warfield or a Jim Stillwagon or one of the other players who came before them.

These young men are embracing the history of Ohio State and its tradition. Now they've created their own memorable part of the proud Buckeye legacy.

The story of the 2002 team is outlined in this book. I hope you enjoy it.

Rex Kern led Ohio State to the 1968 national title, its last before 2002. The Lancaster native now lives in California.

A look back:
Chemistry key part of 1968 national champions

By Jay Hansen
Newspaper Network of Central Ohio

Woody Hayes was well-known as a skilled motivator, coach and teacher. It turns out he was quite a chemist, too.

A chemist? Why not? How else can you explain welding the widely varied talents of Ohio State's 1968 football team into a national champion?

Sure, those Buckeyes had superior talent, but so have many other teams that never won a national championship.

"I think the main ingredient we had working for us was our chemistry," said Jim Otis, a starting fullback on the 1968 squad. "Woody just happened to pick a bunch of kids who cared about each other. We were all great friends."

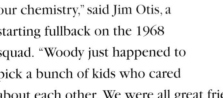

Jay Hansen

Added linebacker Jim Stillwagon: "We had a lot of good chemistry on that team."

To find out the genesis of this chemistry, you have to go back to the 1967 season. That was not a banner year for Ohio State. The Buckeyes were a respectable 6-3, but suffered a humiliating 41-6 loss at home against Purdue.

The year was not without benefit. On the practice fields, a highly regarded freshman class was emerging. Freshmen were not allowed to play in those days, which relegated OSU's talented class to a scout-team role.

The role served as a precursor.

"We were the scout team for the varsity and we gave them all they wanted," Stillwagon said. "They knew we had talent."

This knowledge carried over to 1968, when the Buckeyes' "Super Sophs" exploded onto the college football scene.

Twelve sophomores worked themselves into the starting rotation that season. That class eventually produced six All-Americans, nine all-Big Ten players and 13 NFL draft picks.

"The sophomores came in and raised the bar a bit," Otis said. "They walked to the beat of a different drummer. They went out and had a lot of fun so we went out and had a lot of fun. They had great attitudes, and they all expected to play and win."

The upperclassmen's acceptance of the sophomores was one of the key elements in the Buckeyes' success. This eventual mixing of experienced savvy and youthful exuberance gave the Buckeyes the right mix.

"What made our team special was the way Woody and his coaching staff and the upperclassmen accepted us without reservation," said Rex Kern, who started at quarterback as a sophomore for OSU in 1968. "With our juniors' and seniors' maturity and leadership, they helped keep us intact. We had synergy."

The nation learned how cohesive the group was when the unbeaten Buckeyes played host to No. 1 Purdue the third week of the season.

The Boilermakers had a high-powered offense led by quarterback Mike Phipps and running back Leroy Keyes, and a stout defense to boot. But Ohio State had talent, chemistry and a burr in its saddle from the previous season's shellacking.

"Purdue had embarrassed our varsity the year before and we sat in the stands and watched that," Kern said. "We remembered how that feeling bothered us."

It was all the motivation OSU needed. Ohio State rolled to a 13-0 win, shutting down Keyes and harassing Phipps all afternoon.

"We dominated that game," Otis said.

The Purdue contest was Ohio State's national coming-out party. After the win, OSU romped over Northwestern, then beat Illinois 31-24 after leading 24-0 at halftime. The Buckeyes whipped No. 16 Michigan State, Wisconsin and Iowa in subsequent weeks heading into the annual showdown with Michigan.

During this time, the Buckeyes were continuing to learn and develop the chemistry that made the team great.

"The important thing was we didn't know we were making history at the time," Kern said. "We just went game by game, tried to correct our mistakes and build on what we learned.

"You know, if you're making history, you're probably making bad history. All we set out to do was be the best we could be and beat the school up north."

The Buckeyes did that, too, breaking away from an early 14-14 tie with 36 unanswered points that sealed a 50-14 win.

The last test for Ohio State was in the Rose Bowl, where USC and Heisman Trophy winner O.J. Simpson waited.

USC led early 10-0, with Simpson ripping off an 80-yard touchdown run.

After that, it was all Buckeyes.

"They had us 10-0. Then I scored a touchdown and then we got a field goal," said Otis, who rushed for 101 yards in the game. "We knew then how the game was going to go. At halftime, we knew we were going to go ahead and beat them pretty good."

They did. Kern threw a pair of touchdown passes in the second half on his way to game MVP honors and a 27-16 Buckeye win.

The victory moved Ohio State to 10-0 and sealed the national championship. It was the school's last outright national title before 2002.

In between, the Buckeyes had their chances but came up short. These missed opportunities reinforced the uniqueness of 1968.

"We just had a special team that year, a special group of guys," Kern said. "You look back on 1968 and realize how special it was. Then you look at the elusive titles for the '69 and '70 teams, and all the great teams Archie (Griffin) played on and some of those talented teams (John) Cooper had. You just come to realize it's a once-in-a-lifetime thing."

A Buckeye buzz fills the air

By Jon Spencer
Newspaper Network of Central Ohio

COLUMBUS — Excitement is in the air at Ohio State. Just ask the ballyhooed freshmen.

Quarterback Justin Zwick is so excited, he verbally committed to the Buckeyes in the summer of 2001 and then spent the next few months wooing other recruits to join him in Columbus.

Tailback Maurice Clarett is so excited, he enrolled at OSU last winter and participated in spring drills with the upperclassmen, getting a leg up on the other rookies.

Linebacker Mike D'Andrea is so excited, he was wide awake at 5 a.m., rarin' to go on the first day of preseason camp.

Fourth-year junior tight end Ben Hartsock remembers being in their shoes. He, too, was part of a heralded recruiting class, reeled in on the heels of Ohio State's No. 2 finish in the 1998 polls.

His youthful enthusiasm, however, has turned into prolonged exasperation.

It seems almost unbelievable, but the Buckeyes have failed to post a Top 25 finish since that 1998 season. They have gone 6-6, 8-4 and 7-5 since — three seasons marred by the erratic leadership of quarterback Steve Bellisari.

"Since I was recruited it's been downhill ... and that's something I don't want to be remembered for, as a player who allowed that to happen," Hartsock said. "As someone who's come up through the ranks, and being one of the veterans on the team, I really want to change that idea and help get us back to that powerhouse level."

Fourth-year quarterback Craig Krenzel believes he's the guy to steer the Buckeyes in that direction, but he's being pushed by fellow junior Scott McMullen — with Zwick breathing down their necks in fall camp after peering over their shoulders at spring practice.

"We haven't really played well enough to be in the Top 25 the last three years," Krenzel said. "Rankings don't really matter, anyway. It's the win-loss record. If we go out and play tough and together, we're going to win a lot of games and the rest will take care of itself."

Krenzel made his first start in last year's 26-20 win at Michigan, leading the Buckeyes to their first victory in Ann Arbor since 1987. That apparently has earned him the right to start the opener against

Above: In spring practice, Craig Krenzel wasn't a lock to be the starting quarterback for the Buckeyes. *(Jason J. Molyet/ Newspaper Network of Central Ohio/ Mansfield News Journal)*

Opposite page: Coach Jim Tressel watches the annual Spring Game. *(Jason J. Molyet/Newspaper Network of Central Ohio/Mansfield News Journal)*

Texas Tech in the Pigskin Classic, but doesn't guarantee he'll still have the job when the rematch with Michigan rolls around on Nov. 23.

"Craig played in maybe a total of two games last year," second-year coach Jim Tressel said. "Even if a guy like (middle linebacker) Matt Wilhelm plays in 12 games, if he doesn't perform, he's not going to keep his job.

"Does Matt have a leg up? Sure he does. But you have to perform. It's an ongoing decision. We'll have to watch and see how it progresses."

The tailback race will be another fun one to chart as the Buckeyes embark on a 13-game regular season, the longest in school history.

Sophomore Lydell Ross (hip flexor injury) and redshirt freshman JaJa Riley (appendectomy) have been slowed in the preseason, which could turn things into The Mo Show — starring Maurice "Mo" Clarett and sophomore Maurice "Mo" Hall.

Those two racked up 5,251 rushing yards and 89 touchdowns as seniors — in high school.

"I think we can win with all four tailbacks," running backs coach Tim Spencer said. "They can run and they're all pretty physical. They'll hit you."

It may not matter who's playing

Below: Maurice Clarett, who became the first true freshman to start his first game at running back for Ohio State, works out during spring practice. *(Jason J. Molyet/ Newspaper Network of Central Ohio/ Mansfield News Journal)*

tailback if the Buckeyes don't put things together on the offensive line. A back injury to veteran guard Adrien Clarke limited his practice time in camp. That is a major concern to a unit that must replace All-America center LeCharles Bentley and All-Big Ten tackle Tyson Walter.

The line's development is critical, given that OSU is breaking in an all-new backfield. Gone is three-year starting fullback Jamar Martin, so invaluable as a blocker that it likely will take two players — Branden Joe and Brandon Schnittker — to replace him. Joe will miss the opener as part of his suspension for being charged with DUI.

Depth isn't a problem at wide receiver or among the defensive front seven.

Wide receivers Michael Jenkins (49 catches, 988 yards) and Chris Vance (34 catches, 605 yards) are coming off breakout seasons, and no fewer than seven other wideouts are behind them, itching to provide a breather.

The defense should be quicker, thanks to the development of ends Will Smith and Darrion Scott and the conversion of cornerback Cie Grant to outside linebacker.

All-Big Ten candidate Tim Anderson anchors the defensive front, while All-American Mike Doss and fourth-year starter Donnie Nickey share that distinction from their safety spots.

The OSU staff is leaning heavily on Doss and Nickey to provide guidance for the unproven cornerbacks. Former safety Dustin Fox will start at one corner and Richard McNutt, if he can withstand a chronic ankle problem, appears to be the choice on the other side.

"If we were picking two guys off the street to play cornerback, I'd be concerned," Doss said. "But we know they all have talent and it's their time to step up to the challenge."

Tressel says it's Mike Nugent's time as well. While former walk-on Andy Groom became one of the nation's best punters last season, Nugent and fellow freshman Josh Huston bombed as OSU's two-headed placekicker, converting only 10 of 24 field goal attempts.

Nugent, for reasons that aren't clear, has separated himself from Huston in the battle for that job.

"I think Mike Nugent is going to be a darn good kicker," Tressel said. "Everyone has to go through their freshman year. It's your first time out there in a Big Ten stadium, and everyone needs that growing-up process."

The 2002 forecasters believe the Buckeyes grew up enough in their first season under Tressel to make a serious run at a Big Ten title.

They have 14 starters returning to a team that lost three games by a total of eight points last season.

They also see a squad that was in title contention for the first nine games last season, until Bellisari's arrest and suspension for DUI.

So maybe the pundits are on to something. And maybe the Lou Holtz theory will pan out.

The legendary coach told a banquet crowd in Cleveland earlier this year that during a coaching transition a team makes its greatest improvement in the second season.

"It was true at Youngstown State when we went through it," Tressel said. "We went from 2-9 my first year to 8-4 the next.

"But when I was at Syracuse (as an assistant), we were a transition team and went from 4-6-1 to 3-8, so that wasn't true that time.

"I'm not sure anything is always true. We've got to earn whatever is going to happen. I would like to think we're going to show marked improvement. Will it be reflected in our win-loss record? That's why we're going to line up 13 times."

Left: Coach Jim Tressel watches action during spring practice. *(Jason J. Molyet/Newspaper Network of Central Ohio/Mansfield News Journal)*

OSU looks like well-oiled machine in season-opening win vs. Texas Tech

By Jon Spencer
Newspaper Network of Central Ohio

COLUMBUS — It was the earliest start ever to an Ohio State football season, but the Pigskin Classic found the Buckeyes in midseason form.

Make that mid-1996 form.

It's been six years since OSU advanced to the Rose Bowl, but a few more victories like the season-opening 45-21 rout of Texas Tech will have Buckeye fanatics booking season-ending flights to Pasadena.

A team supposedly rocked early in the week by the suspension of four players appeared not the least bit distracted as it rolled up 477 yards of offense, slowed Tech's pass-happy attack with seven sacks, and threw an unforgettable coming-out party for freshman tailback Maurice Clarett.

Clarett, accustomed to early starts as a Buckeye, rushed for 175 yards and three touchdowns in his debut, added 30 yards in receptions and, perhaps most impressively, didn't get stopped once in the backfield on his 21 carries.

Enrolling at OSU last winter so he could participate in spring drills and get a head start on his college career obviously paid off for the Youngstown native.

Opposite page: Running back Maurice Clarett is congratulated by teammates Ryan Hamby and Brandon Schnittker after his touchdown run in the first quarter. *(Dante Smith/Newspaper Network of Central Ohio/Zanesville Times Recorder)*

Left: Freshman OSU linebacker Bobby Carpenter celebrates a tackle deep in Red Raider territory on the opening kickoff. *(Jason J. Molyet/Newspaper Network of Central Ohio/Mansfield News Journal)*

Clarett raised eyebrows when he criticized the Buckeyes' lack of effort and intensity in practice. His bluntness could have come back to bite him had he not come through like a seasoned veteran against Tech.

"I can't call what I did after one game a success," he said humbly. "If you do this consistently over an entire season then you can call it success."

The 6-foot, 230-pound Clarett knows he can't afford to take his foot off the throttle. Sophomore tailbacks Lydell Ross (40 yards rushing, two TDs) and Maurice Hall (74 yards rushing) are anxious to play more than complementary roles.

"(Fans) love you today, but they may hate you tomorrow," Clarett said. "I'll take what I did with a grain of salt, go back to practice and try to do the best I can."

Usually, it would be easy to call Clarett's performance the difference in the game. His 59-yard burst over an overloaded right side pushed OSU's lead to 14-0 in the first quarter and his carbon-copy jaunt of 45 yards on the fourth snap of the second half put the Red Raiders in a 28-7 bind.

But the defense provided some pivotal plays as well. Middle linebacker Matt Wilhelm proved he's completely recovered from reconstructive ankle surgery by making a team-high nine tackles, none more important than the wallop he put on running back Foy Munlin at the goal line on fourth down. That preserved a 21-7 OSU lead at halftime.

Below, left: Texas Tech's Joselio Hanson and Rodney McKinney try to slow Buckeye freshman running back Maurice Clarett. *(Jason J. Molyet/Newspaper Network of Central Ohio/Mansfield News Journal)*

Below, right: Lydell Ross looks for running room. *(Jason J. Molyet/ Newspaper Network of Central Ohio/Mansfield News Journal)*

Tech coach Mike Leach knew he'd be second-guessed for eschewing a chip-shot field goal on fourth and one.

"You have to be able to get six inches," Leach said. "Give Ohio State a lot of credit. They played well on both sides of the ball. They really didn't do anything we didn't prepare for. They just played well."

Above: Maurice Hall pushes ahead for yards. *(Jason J. Molyet/Newspaper Network of Central Ohio/Mansfield News Journal)*

Left: OSU coach Jim Tressel watches game action. *(Jason J. Molyet/ Newspaper Network of Central Ohio/ Mansfield News Journal)*

Leach and fifth-year quarterback Kliff Kingsbury were hoping to exploit OSU's young cornerbacks. The Raiders capitalized once when Richard McNutt slipped covering Carlos Francis on a fourth-and-two slant route. Once McNutt lost his footing, Francis had clear sailing for a 37-yard TD, cutting the Buckeyes' advantage to 14-7.

But Tech wasn't heard from again until Ohio State was safely in front 38-7, partly because of corner Dustin Fox's interception at the goal line in the third period.

Tech wide receiver Nehemiah Glover worked free in the left

Above: Buckeyes Will Smith and Robert Reynolds show their frustration after Smith dropped an easy interception.
(Jason J. Molyet/Newspaper Network of Central Ohio/Mansfield News Journal)

Right: Linebacker Cie Grant pulls Texas Tech's Mickey Peters out of bounds. *(Jason J. Molyet/Newspaper Network of Central Ohio/Mansfield News Journal)*

corner of the end zone, but Fox recovered to making a diving catch of Kingsbury's floater, preventing Tech from cutting into OSU's 28-7 lead.

"I hope today took some doubts about us away," said Fox, speaking for McNutt. "I felt comfortable out there, and I think this will give Richard and me some confidence."

Left: Buckeye quarterback Craig Krenzel throws deep. *(Jason J. Molyet/Newspaper Network of Central Ohio/Mansfield News Journal)*

If Kingsbury (26 of 44, 341 yards, three TDs) is a Heisman Trophy candidate, what does that make counterpart Craig Krenzel?

Krenzel was a model of efficiency as an opening-day pitcher, completing 11 of 14 passes for 118 yards and orchestrating six scores. He scrambled for 34 yards, didn't throw an interception and showed good poise

Below: Matt Wilhelm and Cie Grant tackle Texas Tech running back Taurean Henderson.
(Kevin Graff/Newspaper Network of Central Ohio/Newark Advocate)

Above: Matt Wilhelm brings down Texas Tech quarterback Kliff Kingsbury.
(Jason J. Molyet/Newspaper Network of Central Ohio/Mansfield News Journal)

Below: OSU coach Jim Tressel and the Buckeyes hold the Pigskin Classic trophy.
(Jason J. Molyet/Newspaper Network of Central Ohio/Mansfield News Journal)

on third-down conversions that led to touchdowns on OSU's first two series of the game.

"Probably what was best about Craig was what was best about the rest of the team," coach Jim Tressel said. "He played the role he needs to play to make us a better football team."

Texas Tech vs #12 Ohio State						
(Aug. 24, 2002 at Columbus, Ohio)						
Score by Quarters	1	2	3	4	Score	
Texas Tech	7	0	0	14	21	Record: (0-1)
Ohio State	14	7	17	7	45	Record: (1-0)

Above: Coach Jim Tressel and the Buckeyes sing "Carmen Ohio" after the game. *(Kevin Graff/ Newspaper Network of Central Ohio/ Newark Advocate)*

CHAPTER THREE ~ SEPTEMBER 7, 2002

Buckeyes roll early in easy win over Kent State

By Jon Spencer
Newspaper Network of Central Ohio

COLUMBUS — Early in the second quarter of Saturday's 51-17 blowout of Kent State, Ohio State safety and senior co-captain Donnie Nickey looked at the faces in the huddle and realized he was surrounded by freshmen.

How weird was that?

"I don't know how weird it was," Nickey said, smiling, "but it was definitely early."

The game started at noon, so some Ohio State fans were still digesting breakfast when Nickey's left hand deflected a Kent State punt that lead to Maurice Clarett's two-yard touchdown run less than three minutes into the game.

When Nickey's sidekick, Mike Doss, intercepted a pass on the ensuing series and returned it 45 yards for a score, the rout was on and OSU's backups

wisely began reaching for their helmets.

The knockout blow was the one-two punch of Nickey and Doss, regarded in some circles as the best safety tandem in the nation.

"What do I call that?" said Nickey, when asked to

Left: Ohio State freshman linebacker A.J. Hawk is all by himself as he returns an interception for a touchdown in the second quarter. *(Jeff Groves/Newspaper Network of Central Ohio/Newark Advocate)*

Right: OSU quarterback Craig Krenzel fires a pass for a first down during the first quarter.
(Jeff Groves/Newspaper Network of Central Ohio/Newark Advocate)

describe their tag-team exploits. "I don't know … I guess I call it good football."

There was plenty of that from the eighth-ranked Buckeyes (2-0). In the first 23 minutes they built a 38-0 lead, helped along by two Clarett touchdowns, a 28-yard scoring burst by Maurice Hall, Craig Krenzel's first TD pass of the season (a seven-yarder to Clarett) and the first of Mike Nugent's three field goals.

Capping the splurge was a 34-yard interception return by freshman A.J. Hawk with 7:31 to play in the second quarter. Hawk was one of 14 true or redshirt freshmen to play against the Golden Flashes (1-1) as coach Jim Tressel took advantage of the lopsided score and overmatched

opponent to empty his bench.

"Any time you can make a big play on special teams, there's electricity in that," Tressel said. "The blocked punt by Donnie was the catalyst, and scoring twice on defense was a big bonus."

Kent had to settle for moral victories. The Flashes outscored OSU 17-13 over the final 37 minutes and held the ball nearly twice as long (39:12 minutes to 20:48) behind multi-threat quarterback Joshua Cribbs.

Cribbs rushed for 94 yards and threw for 160 with two touchdowns, but there was no overcoming his two costly interceptions or Kent's early special teams breakdown.

"No team can spot another team 21 points off the bat like that," Kent coach Dean Pees said. "You can't do that against any team, let alone the eighth-ranked team in the country."

Cribbs' mistakes looked more glaring when weighed against another mistake-free performance by his counterpart.

All Krenzel did was complete his first 11 passes, including the dump-off to Clarett for six points. Krenzel's last pass in the opening 45-21 win over Texas Tech was also a strike, giving him 12 straight completions to tie a school record shared by three other quarterbacks.

How hot was Krenzel?

"It was 90 degrees out there, so I'm guessing he was hot," Tressel deadpanned. "He made good decisions on where to get the ball."

Krenzel finished 12 of 14 passing for 190 yards. He wasn't sacked, didn't throw an interception and played the role of modest hero afterwards.

"It's easy to do your job when you've got a lot of

Below: OSU defensive back Dustin Fox trips up Kent State's Darrell Dowery. *(Ben French/Newspaper Network of Central Ohio/Fremont News-Messenger)*

Right: Kent State quarterback Joshua Cribbs can't vault over linebacker A.J. Hawk. *(Trevor Jones/Newspaper Network of Central Ohio/Coshocton Tribune)*

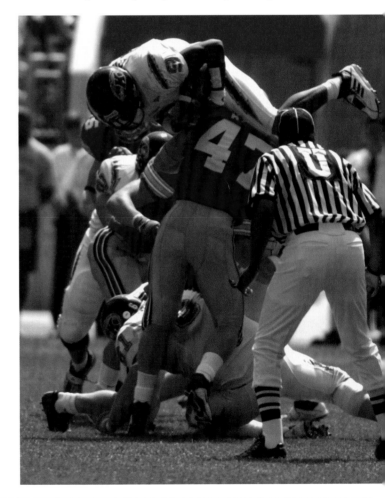

talented receivers running great routes," Krenzel said. "With that kind of combination, it isn't difficult to complete passes."

While Krenzel was nearly perfect, Nugent was absolutely perfect. For the second game in a row he boomed all of his kickoffs into

Above: OSU senior Julie Stachler of Pickerington cools off in the fourth quarter with a bag of ice on her head. Fellow bandmate Shawn Cool of Piqua lends a hand.
(Ben French/Newspaper Network of Central Ohio/Fremont News-Messenger)

Above, right: OSU head coach Jim Tressel ponders a play.
(Trevor Jones/Newspaper Network of Central Ohio/Coshocton Tribune)

Right: Brutus Buckeye cools of in the 90-degree heat before the game.
(Jeff Groves/Newspaper Network of Central Ohio/Newark Advocate)

Below: OSU running back Maurice Clarett runs for a first down during the second quarter. *(Jeff Groves/Newspaper Network of Central Ohio/Newark Advocate)*

the end zone. He also converted field goals of 40, 33 and 45 yards, giving him five straight successful attempts dating back to the end of last season.

"I honestly don't think you can say I have a golden foot," said

Nugent, who has come on strong after a shaky freshman season in 2001. "You could have three or four great games and then fall apart. The key word is consistency. I have to keep this up."

Kent State vs #8 Ohio State						
(Sept. 7, 2002 at Columbus, Ohio)						
Score by Quarters	1	2	3	4	Score	
Kent State	0	14	0	3	17	Record: (1-1)
Ohio State	21	17	3	10	51	Record: (2-0)

Above: OSU's Richard McNutt knocks a pass away from Kent State's Darrell Dowery. *(William P. Cannon/Newspaper Network of Central Ohio/Lancaster Eagle-Gazette)*

Left: Defensive back Nate Salley breaks up a pass in the end zone.
(Trevor Jones/Newspaper Network of Central Ohio/Coshocton Tribune)

Clarett, defense rally Buckeyes past 10th-ranked Washington State

By Jon Spencer
Newspaper Network of Central Ohio

COLUMBUS — If the Ohio State Buckeyes are headed for Pasadena at the end of this football season, they've given every indication they will be flying Clarett Airlines.

In a game billed as a Rose Bowl preview, freshman tailback Maurice Clarett rushed for 230 yards on 31 carries and scored two touchdowns as sixth-ranked OSU rallied past No. 10 Washington State 25-7 before a record Ohio Stadium crowd of 104,553.

Clarett did most of his damage in the second half, racking up 194 yards and both of his TDs on 20 carries. A solid, if unspectacular, defense did the rest as the Buckeyes outscored WSU 19-0 over the last two quarters for their 28th consecutive non-conference win at home.

"He's not a freshman to me," linebacker Matt Wilhelm said of Clarett. "The kid works hard. The benefits he reaps on Saturday he deserves because he works hard Sunday to Friday to get better.

"I take him for granted, but he's a great back. We have a three-headed monster at tailback (with Lydell Ross and Maurice Hall), but he's the one who has risen to the top."

A 44-yard burst around left end by Clarett on the Buckeyes' first play of the third quarter provided lift-off for OSU (3-0) after a turbulent first half. He tacked on a 20-yard gain later in the series,

Opposite page: Buckeye players and fans rejoice after a third-quarter interception by linebacker Matt Wilhelm. *(Dante Smith/Newspaper Network of Central Ohio/Zanesville Times Recorder)*

Left: Maurice Clarett wards off a tackle on his way to a touchdown in the third quarter. *(Jason J. Molyet/Newspaper Network of Central Ohio/Mansfield News Journal)*

careening off two defenders, and then provided the three-yard payoff to erase a 7-6 deficit.

In what has already become "vintage" Clarett, his jaw-dropping display of power and speed accounted for 73 yards on that 91-yard, eight-play drive.

"He makes it easy for us to block and we make it easy for him to run," tight end Ben Hartsock said. "If we give him just a small crease, he can break it off for a big gainer."

Mike Nugent's third field goal, from 45 yards, stretched

Below: Ohio State safety Donnie Nickey chases Washington State quarterback Jason Gesser in the first half. *(Bill Sinden/ Newspaper Network of Central Ohio/Marion Star)*

Right: OSU defensive lineman Kenny Peterson takes down Washington State quarterback Jason Gesser in the second quarter. *(Dante Smith/ Newspaper Network of Central Ohio/Zanesville Times Recorder)*

the lead to 16-7. The Buckeyes then turned a bad snap by WSU in punt formation into a nine-point mistake to all but put the game out of reach.

The botched snap sailed through the end zone for an easy two points with 47 seconds remaining in the third quarter. The Buckeyes then capitalized on the ensuing free kick, driving 66 yards on 10 plays.

Clarett provided the capper from one yard out, even though quarterback Craig Krenzel appeared to lunge into the end zone on his 29-yard keeper one play earlier.

Below: Ohio State punter Andy Groom booms a kick.

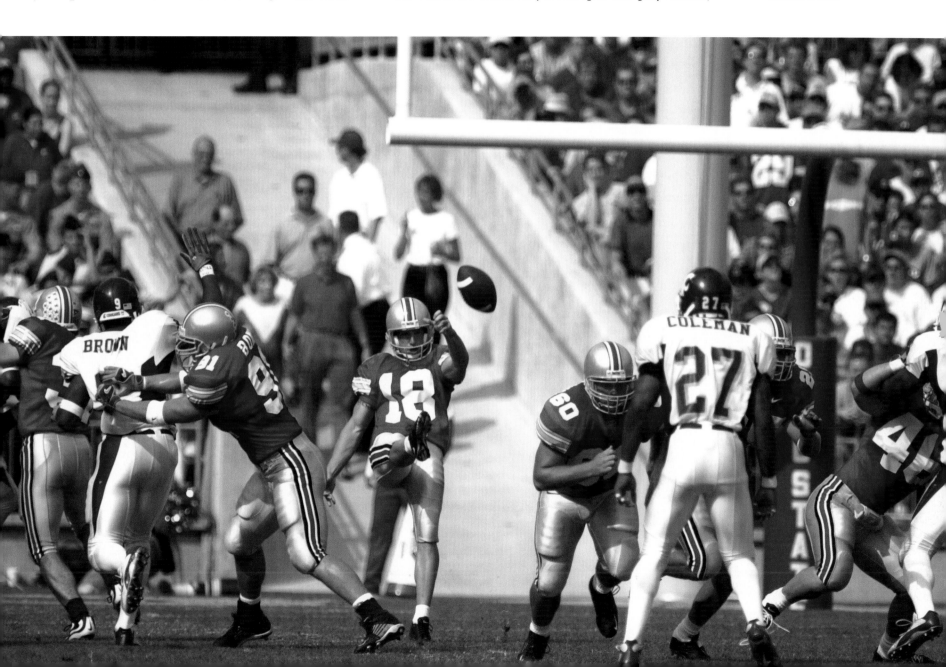

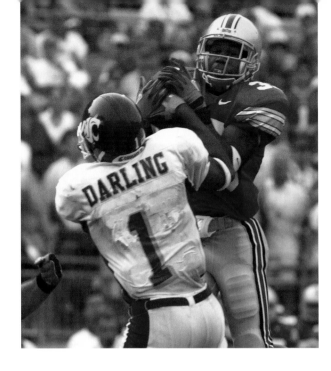

Right: Ohio State's Tyler Everett takes the ball away from Washington State's Devard Darling near the goal line in the fourth quarter. *(Bill Sinden/ Newspaper Network of Central Ohio/ Marion Star)*

Below, left: Craig Krenzel reaches just short of the end zone in the fourth quarter. *(Dante Smith/Newspaper Network of Central Ohio/Zanesville Times Recorder)*

Below, right: Maurice Clarett is off and running in the third quarter. *(Dante Smith/Newspaper Network of Central Ohio/Zanesville Times Recorder)*

Until Clarett sprouted wings, the Buckeyes never left the runway. At halftime they were 0 for 6 on third-down conversions and had 109 yards total offense — 33 of that coming on a pass from quarterback Krenzel to wide-open Michael Jenkins on the game's first play.

That led to the first of Nugent's two 43-yard field goals in the first half. But the Buckeyes never sniffed the end zone before the band show.

"Some of the guys on offense were calling each other out at halftime," Hartsock said. "In other seasons that might have escalated into something bad, but today it just pushed us to the next level."

The OSU defense may have failed to steal Clarett's thunder, but the Buckeyes shut down the Cougars (2-1) after they

drove 80 yards for a touchdown on their opening series.

Despite completing 25 of 44 passes for 247 yards, Heisman Trophy candidate Jason Gesser had trouble stretching the field and was intercepted twice in the second

Above: Cie Grant and #75 Simon Fraser fall on a Washington State fumble in the second quarter. *(Bill Sinden/Newspaper Network of Central Ohio/Marion Star)*

Right: Michael Jenkins hauls in a 33-yard pass from Craig Krenzel on Ohio State's first play of the game. *(Dante Smith/Newspaper Network of Central Ohio/ Zanesville Times Recorder)*

#10 Washington State vs #6 Ohio State (Sept. 14, 2002 at Columbus, Ohio)					
Score by Quarters	1	2	3	4	Score
Washington State	7	0	0	0	7 Record: (2-1)
Ohio State	3	3	12	7	25 Record: (3-0)

Right: OSU's Will Smith and Kenny Peterson celebrate Peterson's sack of Washington State quarterback Jason Gesser in the second quarter. *(Dante Smith/Newspaper Network of Central Ohio/Zanesville Times Recorder)*

Far right: OSU quarterback Craig Krenzel fires a pass in the first half. *(Jason J. Molyet/Newspaper Network of Central Ohio/Mansfield News Journal)*

Below: Donnie Nickey breaks up a pass intended for Washington State's Devard Darling in the second quarter. *(Bill Sinden/Newspaper Network of Central Ohio/Marion Star)*

half — one on a spectacular one-handed grab by middle linebacker Matt Wilhelm. The other, by freshman DB Tyler Everett at the OSU 4, killed a 13-play drive in the final period.

"As we sat there at halftime, we knew that if everyone eliminated their mistakes and played well technique-wise, we were going to have a chance," OSU coach Jim Tressel said. "I felt that if we settled down, we'd have a chance to win the game."

Left: OSU tight end Ben Hartsock raises his arms as OSU head coach Jim Tressel prepares to lead the Buckeyes in "Carmen Ohio" after the game.
(Jason J. Molyet/Newspaper Network of Central Ohio/Mansfield News Journal)

Buckeyes survive landmine in 23-19 win at Cincinnati

By Jon Spencer
Newspaper Network of Central Ohio

CINCINNATI — Tight end Ben Hartsock knew Ohio State's game with 17-point underdog Cincinnati had a chance of blowing up in the Buckeyes' faces.

Never mind the cautionary words he probably heard over and over again from his coaches during the week. The message came through loud and clear over a college football Web site.

"One of them called it one of the non-conference 'landmine' games of the year," said Hartsock, a look of relief on his face after sixth-ranked OSU survived a 23-19 scare from their fiesty hosts.

"People who know football knew this was a dangerous game for us. They knew that everybody in Cincinnati has had this game circled on the calendar for a long time."

It had been even longer since Ohio State last played an in-state road game against an Ohio opponent (1934) and longer than that since the Buckeyes had lost to an Ohio opponent (1921, 7-6 to Oberlin).

But it wasn't until nickel back Will Allen's interception in the end zone, on a tipped fourth-down pass by middle linebacker Matt Wilhelm, that the Buckeyes sealed the victory with 26 seconds left before a city-record crowd of 66,319 in Paul Brown Stadium.

"I was nervous," said Wilhelm, who fell after deflecting the pass, "because a tipped ball is almost like a Hail Mary. But I looked over my shoulder and

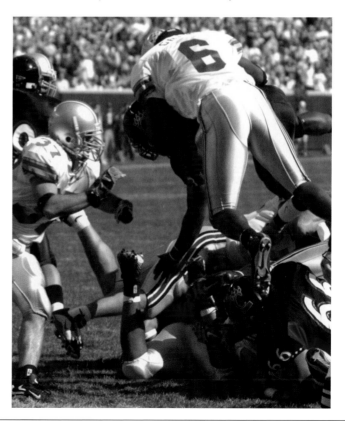

Opposite page: Ohio State's Ivan Douglas (53) and Chris Vance (4) lift quarterback Craig Krenzel after he scored the winning touchdown in the fourth quarter. *(William P. Cannon/Newspaper Network of Central Ohio/Lancaster Eagle-Gazette)*

Left: Ohio State linebacker Cie Grant stops Cincinnati running back DeMarco McCleskey from scoring in the first quarter. McCleskey scored on the next play to give UC a 6-0 lead. *(Dave Polcyn/Newspaper Network of Central Ohio/Mansfield News Journal)*

saw Will make a basket catch."

Playing without freshman sensation Maurice Clarett, the Buckeyes (4-0) beat Cincinnati (1-2) at its own game, scoring nine unanswered points to prove the Cardiac Cats don't have a patent on fourth-quarter comebacks.

The karma appeared to be bad most of the afternoon for the Buckeyes. They came back from a 12-7 halftime deficit to take the lead, only to fall behind 19-14 on a three-yard TD catch by Tye Keith with 2:36 left in the third quarter.

With a chance to take the lead early in the fourth quarter, the Buckeyes were penalized for having 12 men on the field on fourth and goal from the two and had to settle for a 24-yard field goal from Mike Nugent.

That seemed to be playing into the hands of UC's sophomore quarterback Gino Guidugli. Normally he does his best work late, having already engineered four comeback victories in his short career with the Bearcats.

This time, the hero's cape was worn by counterpart Craig Krenzel. While Guidugli threw two interceptions and fumbled once in the final period, Krenzel scored the game-winner with 3:44 to play on a spinning, six-yard run through three defenders that had CLARETT written all over it.

Defensive end Darrion Scott made Krenzel's tremendous run possible by separating Guidugli from the ball on a blind-side sack. Tackle David Thompson recovered the ball at the UC 47.

"We were hoping they'd cover Michael Jenkins man-to-man and we could beat them on a slant route," Krenzel

Below, left: OSU's Darrion Scott sacks UC quarterback Gino Guidugli, causing a fumble in the fourth quarter that led to the Buckeyes' winning touchdown. *(Dave Polcyn/ Newspaper Network of Central Ohio/Mansfield News Journal)*

Below, right: OSU tight end Ben Hartsock dives unsuccessfully for a Craig Krenzel pass. *(William P. Cannon/Newspaper Network of Central Ohio/Lancaster Eagle-Gazette)*

said of the aborted pass play on second and goal. "But I decided at that point to break out of the pocket and make something happen."

Coach Jim Tressel was glad it wasn't something bad.

"It was an excellent effort by Craig, and the best thing about the play is that he didn't try to force (the ball) to someone that wasn't open," Tressel said. "A turnover would have really hurt us there."

Krenzel's TD run capped a performance that saw him negate two first-half interceptions with a pair of second-half TD passes — to Hartsock and flanker Chris Vance. Krenzel also scampered 29 yards to the six to

set up Nugent's field goal, while Lydell Ross rushed for 130 yards on 23 carries in Clarett's absence.

"Any hard-fought victory is a good one," Tressel said. "I'd rather learn lessons that way than after hard-fought losses."

For the second week in a row, the Buckeyes trailed at halftime. They fell behind 9-0 and then 12-7 at the break, and it could have been much worse.

OSU committed three turnovers (two

Above: Cincinnati's Doug Monaghan tries to bring down OSU's Lydell Ross in the third quarter.
(Dave Polcyn/Newspaper Network of Central Ohio/Mansfield News Journal)

Left: OSU's Dustin Fox tackles DeMarco McCleskey after a long run in the first quarter.
(Dave Polcyn/Newspaper Network of Central Ohio/Mansfield News Journal)

interceptions and a fumble) and also had a 96-yard kickoff return by Chris Gamble negated by a holding penalty — all before intermission.

The interceptions, both by cornerback Blue Adams, gave UC possession at its own 45 and the OSU 38, but the Bearcats failed to capitalize on either opportunity.

They also came up empty on a fumble by Maurice Hall at the OSU 37 and settled for a 44-yard field goal by Jonathan Ruffin after a 46-yard burst by tailback DeMarco McClesky had given them a first down at the OSU 18.

But Ohio State wasted field position as well. The

Buckeyes did nothing after Hall returned the opening kickoff 45 yards and then looked helpless as UC took the ensuing punt and drove 80 yards in nine plays for a 7-0 lead.

Guidugli completed passes on the first five plays of the drive and then hit Keith for 36 yards to the one, setting up McClesky's TD on an option pitch. Ruffin missed the PAT, breaking his streak of 65 in a row, but his 44-yard field goal made it 9-0 with 6:24 left in the first quarter.

OSU cut the deficit to 9-7 when Krenzel lobbed a

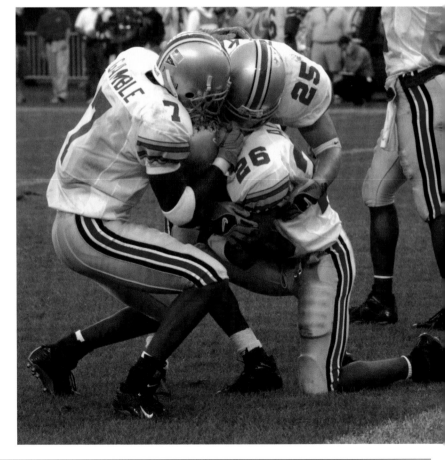

20-yard pass over the middle to wide-open tight end Ben Hartsock, but the Bearcats answered with a 49-yard field goal by Ruffin for their halftime cushion.

"We take no solace in losing," UC coach Rick Minter said. "We had a chance to win and didn't. You never, ever want to be satisfied with losing."

#6 Ohio State vs Cincinnati
(Sept. 21, 2002 at Cincinnati, Ohio)

Score by Quarters	1	2	3	4	Score	
Ohio State	0	7	7	9	23	Record: (4-0)
Cincinnati	9	3	7	0	19	Record: (1-2)

Below: OSU quarterback Craig Krenzel unloads a pass while in the grasp of UC's Tommy Simpson.
(Dave Polcyn/Newspaper Network of Central Ohio/Mansfield News Journal)

OSU offense shows new wrinkles in 45-17 beating of Hoosiers

By Jon Spencer
Newspaper Network of Central Ohio

COLUMBUS — A Jim Tressel-designed offense is usually as cutting edge as that choir boy's necktie-and-sweater vest ensemble he favors on game day.

So imagine everyone's surprise when his unbeaten Ohio State Buckeyes unveiled a spread attack against Indiana, sometimes featuring as many as five receivers out wide with no running backs behind quarterback Craig Krenzel.

What next? Tressel all decked out from head to toe in scarlet and gray leather?

"It's been in our playbook. We just hadn't brought it out yet," split end Michael Jenkins said after the 45-17 rout of the Hoosiers in the Big Ten opener in Ohio Stadium. "I think coach was waiting to bring out the five-wide for the Big Ten season ... a little change-up."

It was more than a little change-up. It was a 100 mph fastball up and in, with the stunned Hoosiers hitting the dirt.

Jenkins caught his first two touchdowns of the season with the Buckeyes (5-0) in a spread alignment, after they had first softened IU with continuous body shots from punishing tailback Maurice Clarett (104 yards rushing, three TDs).

Left: OSU's Darrion Scott, left, Will Smith and Simon Fraser gang-tackle Indiana's Yamar Washington. *(James Miller/Newspaper Network of Central Ohio/Marion Star)*

Right: OSU quarterback Craig Krenzel tries to avoid Indiana's Victor Adeyanju. *(Mike Lehmkuhle/Newspaper Network of Central Ohio/Newark Advocate)*

"Our running game has been going really well, so I knew we weren't going to shy away from that," Jenkins said. "But we needed to get the passing game going, and this (spread) just added to it.

"We try and hint to all the coaches about getting three or four receivers in, so when they call us out there we have to make some plays. Once we got it going, and they had to also defend the run, we could really pick and choose."

The Buckeyes opened the game in a spread, went the more conventional route — Clarett left, Clarett right, Clarett up the middle — to build a little cushion, and then returned to their new-fangled, wide-open ways while scoring 31 unanswered points to break open a 14-10 contest.

"We gave (Indiana) a couple of other things to think about," Tressel

Above: Will Smith sacks Indiana quarterback Gibran Hamdan. *(Christopher Crook/Newspaper Network of Central Ohio/Zanesville Times Recorder)*

Left: Michael Jenkins stretches to catch a pass over Indiana's Duane Stone. *(James Miller/Newspaper Network of Central Ohio/Marion Star)*

said. "I thought over the course of the game our offensive coaches did a pretty good job of mixing in some of their power, bread-and-butter game with some of the other things we're giving (the opposition) to work on.

"(The five-wide) was something we hadn't shown, and that's always hard on defenses, because you're giving them something they hadn't worked on all week.

"I thought our guys did a nice job of pass protecting because you only have five guys for protection when you put five guys out wide. Just in general terms it was good change of pace for us."

Jenkins lined up in the slot before making a four-yard TD catch on a fade route. That's something OSU fans hadn't seen from the Buckeyes. The reverse by flanker Chris Gamble that went for a 43-yard TD was another new wrinkle.

"What you'd like to have is an extraordinary group of running backs

Above: OSU defensive back Dustin Fox breaks up a pass intended for Indiana's Glenn Johnson. *(Jeff Groves/Newspaper Network of Central Ohio/Newark Advocate)*

Left: OSU linebacker Cie Grant tries to strip the ball from Indiana's Aaron Halterman. *(Christopher Crook/Newspaper Network of Central Ohio/Zanesville Times Recorder)*

which, leading with Maurice, I think we do," Tressel said. "But when you can have great backs and outstanding big-play receivers, I think we have the makings of an offense that can strike from a lot of different places."

Krenzel rebounded from a couple of shaky outings to complete 11 of 16 passes (two were dropped) for 152 yards and one TD against Indiana. For the fourth time in five games, he didn't throw an interception.

"(The spread) is definitely exciting; it gets the quarterbacks and wideouts more involved," Krenzel said. "The more we do it, the more consistent we can get with it, and the more confidence we can establish with the coaches, we can go out and get seven or eight yards and sometimes turn it into a big play."

Above: OSU wide receiver Chris Gamble scampers for a first down.
(Mike Lehmkuhle/Newspaper Network of Central Ohio/Newark Advocate)

Right: Buckeye fans celebrate a second-quarter touchdown.
(Jeff Groves/Newspaper Network of Central Ohio/Newark Advocate)

Krenzel's bugaboo remains the deep pass. He badly underthrew Jenkins on OSU's first play from scrimmage after the receiver got open on what could have been an 80-yard scoring bomb.

"We know we can go deep; Craig throws the ball real well during practice," Jenkins said. "It's just that in games he may not realize how fast we are, with all the adrenaline going, and sometimes he underthrows it."

Below: Maurice Clarett reaches for a touchdown over Indiana's A.C. Carter late in the second quarter. *(James Miller/Newspaper Network of Central Ohio/Marion Star)*

Above: OSU's Robert Reynolds and E.J. Underwood tackle Indiana's Yamar Washington. *(Mike Lehmkuhle/Newspaper Network of Central Ohio/Newark Advocate)*

Opposite page: Michael Jenkins catches a Scott McMullen touchdown pass over the outstretched hands of Indiana's Damien Jones. *(Christopher Crook/Newspaper Network of Central Ohio/Zanesville Times Recorder)*

Left: OSU holder Andy Groom congratulates kicker Mike Nugent after he made a 51-yard field goal. *(Mike Lehmkuhle/Newspaper Network of Central Ohio/Newark Advocate)*

Indiana vs #6 Ohio State
(Sept. 28, 2002 at Columbus, Ohio)

Score by Quarters	1	2	3	4	Score	
Indiana	0	10	0	7	17	Record: (2-3,0-1)
Ohio State	7	14	17	7	45	Record: (5-0,1-0)

Clarett struggles, but OSU gets ugly 27-16 road win

By Jon Spencer
Newspaper Network of Central Ohio

EVANSTON, Ill. — Maurice Clarett has to be thankful his first plane trip with the Ohio State Buckeyes is over.

A turbulent week found the freshman phenom admitting his fear of flying and then looking just as jittery on the ground in a 27-16 victory at Northwestern.

Clarett overcame three fumbles to score two touchdowns and gain more than 100 yards rushing for the fourth time in five starts this season as the fifth-ranked Buckeyes (6-0, 2-0) handed the Wildcats (2-4, 0-2) their 22nd consecutive loss in this series.

A 20-yard TD run by Clarett in the third quarter seemed to put the Buckeyes safely in front 24-9. But it wasn't until a Cie Grant interception negated Clarett's third fumble late in the game that OSU could begin to celebrate.

"Offensively, you always have to be mistake-free on the road," coach Jim Tressel said. "You cannot go on the road, make mistakes and win in the Big Ten — and we turned it over three times.

"We've got to be better on the road. There is no way we win our next away game if we keep making

Left: Northwestern defenders bring down Michael Jenkins after a second-quarter catch. *(William P. Cannon/Newspaper Network of Central Ohio/Lancaster Eagle-Gazette)*

Right: Maurice Clarett breaks away for yardage. *(William P. Cannon/Newspaper Network of Central Ohio/Lancaster Eagle-Gazette)*

some of the same mistakes."

Clarett finished with 140 yards on 29 carries. But in a stunning reversal of roles, Northwestern's beleaguered defense came out looking superhuman while Clarett went from looking stupendous so far this season to just plain stupefying.

He has now lost four fumbles on 113 carries.

"Horrible," Clarett said, describing his performance. "We won, though. I would have basically been the reason we lost if we lost. (The 140 rushing yards) doesn't really mean nothing when you have three fumbles."

Clarett's run to the Heisman Trophy hit an unforeseen roadblock as the nation's second-worst run defense forced him

Right: Buckeye Mike Doss breaks up a pass intended for Northwestern's Ashton Aikens in the second quarter. *(William P. Cannon/ Newspaper Network of Central Ohio/ Lancaster Eagle-Gazette)*

Below: Ohio State's Maurice Clarett talks to head coach Jim Tressel after the freshman fumbled for the third time. *(William P. Cannon/ Newspaper Network of Central Ohio/ Lancaster Eagle-Gazette)*

to fumble the ball away twice — at the OSU 44 and then at the OSU nine after a punt had pinned the Buckeyes deep.

Northwestern capitalized only on the second turnover, and even then had to settle for a 26-yard David Wasielewski field goal and a 3-0 lead.

Ohio State had a chance to go in front on the ensuing possession, but was stopped on fourth and two at the NU 26. This time Clarett held on to the ball, but he got stonewalled for no gain by cornerback Hershel Henderson.

The Wildcats made it 6-0 with 58 seconds left in the first quarter on a 27-yard field goal by Wasielewski, but OSU answered with a 66-

Left: Ohio State's Lydell Ross sizes up Northwestern's Doug Szymul. *(William P. Cannon/ Newspaper Network of Central Ohio/Lancaster Eagle-Gazette)*

Below: Northwestern's Doug Szymul closes in on Ohio State's Craig Krenzel. *(William P. Cannon/ Newspaper Network of Central Ohio/ Lancaster Eagle-Gazette)*

yard, six-play drive that featured 51 yards in completions by quarterback Craig Krenzel and his own 12-yard scramble to the NU seven. That set up the three-yard payoff by Lydell Ross, giving the Buckeyes a 7-6 lead.

Wasielewski's third field goal — a 37-yarder — regained the lead for Northwestern, but it could have been worse for OSU. That series began with a personal foul for unnecessary roughness by the Wildcats, negating a 78-yard punt return by Kunle Patrick to the OSU nine.

On that same drive, a 21-yard TD pass from quarterback

Brett Basanez to Reynoldsburg, Ohio, native Mark Philmore was waved off when the officials ruled that Philmore did not have possession of the ball before falling out of the end zone. TV replays appeared to show otherwise.

OSU went back in front 14-9 on its next possession. Chris Gamble caught a 48-yard bomb from Krenzel that carried to the NU 15 and set up Clarett's two-yard payoff with 2:37 left in the half.

A goal-line stand by the Buckeyes preserved their

Above: Ohio State student Chad Sakada, 20, of Kettering, Ohio, cheers after Cie Grant's fourth-quarter interception. *(William P. Cannon/ Gannett News Service/Lancaster Eagle-Gazette)*

Left: Northwestern's Matt Ulrich and Eric Worley chase Ohio State's Cie Grant after he intercepted a pass by Wildcat quarterback Brett Basanez in the fourth quarter. *(William P. Cannon/Gannett News Service/Lancaster Eagle-Gazette)*

lead at halftime. They stopped NU on two cracks from the one and the Wildcats were foiled completely when Wasielewski's 18-yard field goal attempt sailed wide right.

"Northwestern put together a great scheme on defense," tight end Ben Hartsock. "They had us guessing the whole game.

"I know Maurice is going to be frustrated because he's a competitor like the rest of us. He should be frustrated."

Above: Ohio State's Mike Doss (2) and Darrion Scott (56) try to block a Northwestern field goal in the first quarter.
(William P. Cannon/Gannett News Service/Lancaster Eagle-Gazette)

#5 Ohio State vs Northwestern
(Oct. 5, 2002 at Evanston, Ill.)

Score by Quarters	1	2	3	4	Score	
Ohio State	0	14	10	3	27	Record: (6-0,2-0)
Northwestern	6	3	7	0	16	Record: (2-4,0-2)

CHAPTER EIGHT ~ OCTOBER 12, 2002

OSU passing attack gets in gear during 50-7 win vs. San Jose State

By Jon Spencer
Newspaper Network of Central Ohio

COLUMBUS — With a sensational tailback behind him, practically demanding the football, Ohio State quarterback Craig Krenzel knew there was no way — statistically — he and his receiving corps could keep up with the aerial circus San Jose State brought into Ohio Stadium.

Yet there was Krenzel at the wheel of the getaway car.

Answering criticism about his inability to throw deep, Krenzel fired two long touchdown passes and an even longer strike that led to a field goal as the fifth-ranked Buckeyes blew past the Spartans 50-7 before a record Homecoming crowd of 104,892.

While San Jose State had little to show for Scott Rislov's school-record 36 completions, Krenzel made the most of his modest 14 passing attempts, completing 11 for 241 yards and three touchdowns. Two dropped passes and a throw-away spoiled an otherwise perfect day for the cool-headed junior.

"We see this from him all the time in practice," said split end Michael Jenkins after catching seven passes for 136 yards and a TD. "It's a matter of

evolving and getting the chemistry down with the receivers.

"Once you start completing the deep passes, that

Opposite page: Ohio State's Chris Vance and Michael Jenkins bump chests after Vance hauled in the Buckeyes' second touchdown against San Jose State. *(Dante Smith/Newspaper Network of Central Ohio/Zanesville Times Recorder)*

Left: Michael Jenkins burns the San Jose State secondary for a 40-yard touchdown in the third quarter. *(James Miller/Newspaper Network of Central Ohio/Marion Star)*

Above: San Jose State defenders tackle receiver Chris Gamble. *(Dante Smith/ Newspaper Network of Central Ohio/ Zanesville Times Recorder)*

Above, right: Matt Wilhelm and David Thompson make a diving stop on San Jose State's Charles Pauley. *(Trevor Jones/Newspaper Network of Central Ohio/Coshocton Tribune)*

Right: Ohio State's Cie Grant drags down Charles Pauley for a loss. *(Dante Smith/Newspaper Network of Central Ohio/Zanesville Times Recorder)*

gets the defense thinking and opens things up for our running game."

Freshman Maurice Clarett handled (pardon the pun) that part of the attack, rushing for 132 yards and two touchdowns on 18 carries. More importantly, he didn't fumble against the nation's top team in takeaways after fumbling three times in the previous game, a 27-16 victory at Northwestern.

Clarett even contributed to the air assault, soaring over a defender and across the goal line while turning a dump-off from Krenzel into an acrobatic seven-yard score.

That touchdown was sandwiched between a 40-yard field goal by Mike Nugent and a 40-yard TD catch by Jenkins as the Buckeyes (7-0) scored 17 points in the first 6:24 of the third quarter to put the game out of reach 41-7.

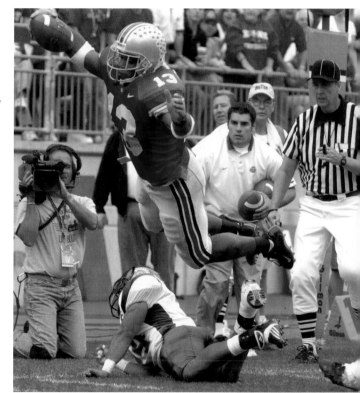

Above: Ohio State's Chris Vance hauls in the Buckeyes' second touchdown, a 37-yard pass from Craig Krenzel, in the second quarter. *(Dante Smith/Newspaper Network of Central Ohio/Zanesville Times Recorder)*

Left: Brutus Buckeye leads the charge as Ohio State takes the field. *(Trevor Jones/Newspaper Network of Central Ohio/ Coshocton Tribune)*

Right: Maurice Clarett leaps over a San Jose State defender for a touchdown in the third quarter. *(David Distlehorst/Newspaper Network of Central Ohio/ Newark Advocate)*

A 47-yard bomb from Krenzel to Chris Gamble set up the Nugent field goal, and back-to-back fumbles by Spartan wideouts led to Krenzel's two touchdown passes in the period. The latter was a perfectly threaded bullet to Jenkins between two defenders.

Jenkins didn't have to come back for the long ball, as had often been the case this season. Chris Vance didn't, either, on his finger-tip grab for a 37-yard score in the second quarter.

"It's been frustrating to us, to have so many big-play guys and not be throwing the ball downfield with success," Krenzel said. "I knew we were only a split-second away in our timing from getting things turned around."

The Krenzel-to-Vance hookup was big, coming

moments after the Spartans (4-3) closed to within 10-7 on a nine-yard pass from Rislov to Charles Pauley.

But San Jose State wasn't ready to fold — yet. The Spartans quickly moved downfield on eight completions by Rislov and were poised to strike from the OSU 10. But linebacker Cie Grant came swooping in on first down to sack Rislov, jarring the ball loose. Freshman end Mike

Below, left: Ohio State's David Thompson pursues San Jose State's Lance Martin. *(David Distlehorst/ Newspaper Network of Central Ohio/Newark Advocate)*

Below, right: San Jose State defenders bring down Buckeye quarterback Craig Krenzel in the second half. *(David Distlehorst/ Newspaper Network of Central Ohio/Newark Advocate)*

Kudla, spelling the injured Will Smith (knee sprain), picked up the fumble and returned it 17 yards to the OSU 41.

That paved the way for Clarett's five-yard run for a 24-7 lead, which the Buckeyes preserved at halftime after Spartan wideout Tuati Wooden fumbled at the OSU 24 as time expired.

Known for their takeaways (15 interceptions, nine fumble recoveries), the Spartans played giveaway against the Buckeyes, fumbling on their last two possessions of the second quarter and first two series of the second half. Those mistakes led to three TDs by Ohio State, which committed its only turnover — a fumble by Drew Carter — after the outcome was decided.

Throwing mostly swing

Left: Ohio State's Michael Jenkins celebrates with Chris Gamble and Ben Hartsock after scoring a touchdown in the third quarter. *(James Miller/Newspaper Network of Central Ohio/Marion Star)*

San Jose State vs #5 Ohio State
(Oct. 12, 2002 at Columbus, Ohio)

Score by Quarters	1	2	3	4	Score	
San Jose State	0	7	0	0	7	Record: (4-3)
Ohio State	7	17	17	9	50	Record: (7-0)

passes and screens, Rislov was 31 of 37 for 257 yards by halftime. But he threw for just eight yards in the third quarter before getting yanked. His replacement, Marcus Arroyo, didn't complete a pass as the Spartans finished with only 15 yards total offense in the second half — and got outgained 212 to 0 on the ground overall.

"In the first half, we did everything that we wanted to do; we just didn't get the ball in the end zone the way we thought we would," San Jose State coach Fitz Hill said. "We thought we could play with them on the perimeter, but we gave up too many turnovers."

Above: San Jose State's Charles Pauley is mugged by Ohio State's Jason Bond (91) and Dustin Fox (37). *(James Miller/Newspaper Network of Central Ohio/Marion Star)*

Opposite page: San Jose State punter Michael Carr is roughed by Will Smith (93) in the first half. *(James Miller/Newspaper Network of Central Ohio/Marion Star)*

Below: Buckeye defenders chase San Jose State's Charles Pauley. *(James Miller/Newspaper Network of Central Ohio/Marion Star)*

Wilhelm pushing himself harder — with help from Doss

By Jon Spencer
Newspaper Network of Central Ohio

COLUMBUS — A healthy and rejuvenated Matt Wilhelm has restored order at the top of the tackle chart at Ohio State — and made a betting man of teammate Mike Doss.

"He got after me in the weight room this past Sunday and had obviously seen a stat sheet," said Wilhelm, who leads the fourth-ranked Buckeyes in tackles, by a 56-48 margin over Doss, entering their game at Wisconsin.

Right: OSU linebacker Matt Wilhelm jumps in front of a pass by Texas Tech's Kliff Kingsbury as defensive lineman Darrion Scott closes in during the Buckeyes' season opening win vs. the Red Raiders. *(Jason J. Molyet/Newspaper Network of Central Ohio/Mansfield News Journal)*

"He isn't too pleased with that. We actually have a friendly bet going right now, for dinner or something. He said he's not going to get beat out as the team's leading tackler after leading for two years straight."

Watching middle linebackers — like Wilhelm — lead the Buckeyes in tackles once was as much of an OSU tradition as Woody Hayes shredding sideline markers and sousaphone players dotting the "i" in Script Ohio.

But the balance of power shifted in recent seasons to the secondary, with defensive backs finishing on top of the tackle chart five of the past six years. Wilhelm is halfway to bucking that trend and is on pace to become the first OSU linebacker to record 100 tackles since Lorenzo Styles had 132 in 1994.

The wager between Wilhelm and Doss is a no-lose proposition for the Buckeyes if it means those two defensive leaders continue to step up their games as OSU enters the most challenging stretch of its season.

"It's all in good fun," Wilhelm said. "It's two great football players pushing each other. When the game is on the line, I'm going to run after the football and make the tackle just to stay one up on Mike Doss."

Running to the football was something that became increasingly difficult last season for Wilhelm after he tore three ligaments in his right ankle against Northwestern. He missed only the next game, against Wisconsin, but his mobility was obviously hampered the rest of the season as he lost the team lead in tackles and finished third behind Doss and linebacker Joe Cooper.

Wilhelm opted to have reconstructive surgery after the season rather than rehab and come back at 90 percent this season. It meant sitting out spring ball, but it was a move he hasn't regretted.

"The ankle has not bothered me one bit," said the 6-5, 245-pound senior, who leads the Big Ten with 11 tackles for loss. "Sitting out the spring was 15 days of pounding taken off my body."

Wilhelm worked on his conditioning and pushed himself mentally, studying the intricacies of the game and taking to heart a film compiled by linebackers coach Mark Snyder that showed all of Wilhelm's missed tackles from last year — as well as 10 examples of him not pursuing the ball.

"I've improved my tackling and relentless pursuit of the football," Wilhelm said. "I've gotten a lot of charity tackles just by running to the football from sideline to sideline."

Wilhelm's name is attached to two of the biggest defensive plays of the season by the unbeaten Buckeyes (7-0, 2-0 in the Big Ten).

Against Washington State, he checked out of a blitz and tipped a pass that he caught falling down, blunting a Cougars' drive in the third quarter. The following week at Cincinnati, with the Bearcats throwing into the end zone from the OSU 15 on the game's final play, Wilhelm tipped a potential TD pass into the hands of safety Will Allen.

"Matt has really stepped up his game," defensive tackle Kenny Peterson said. "He's shocked a lot of people. He's become a lot more aggressive. He's making some great plays out there."

The first sign that Wilhelm was all the way back came in the opener against Texas Tech. On a fourth-down play at the goal line, Wilhelm stuffed running back Foy Munlin for no gain, stopping a drive that would have cut the Buckeyes' lead to a touchdown. They went on to win 45-21.

He made a similar play last week against San Jose State, catching running back Trestin George in the backfield on fourth down on the game's opening series.

"It's our hope that everyone entering their senior year has one of those career-best years," head coach Jim Tressel said. "Matt didn't get to play as much in the spring as he would have liked to, and some guys would have allowed that to set them back a little bit. But he took that opportunity to learn the game even more, although his knowledge of football was already extraordinary.

"He trained hard and did what he had to do to prepare for an extraordinary senior year. He's halfway there."

When fall camp opened, Wilhelm found Fred Pagac Jr. listed as a co-starter at middle linebacker. He also had to listen to speculation that freshman Mike D'Andrea, a Parade high school All-American, would take his job.

"It obviously fueled my work ethic," Wilhelm said. "That's the reason you stay an extra half-hour to get on the treadmill and run that extra mile."

CHAPTER NINE ~ OCTOBER 19, 2002

Buckeyes clamp down in second half, top Badgers 19-14

By Jon Spencer
Newspaper Network of Central Ohio

MADISON, Wis. — There was no dancing on the "W" by the Ohio State Buckeyes after their 19-14 victory over Wisconsin. But a couple of "thank you" prayers from the midfield logo might have been a nice touch.

Trailing 14-13 early in the fourth quarter with his team facing third and six from the OSU 16, Michael Jenkins went up for a Hail Mary-like pass from Craig Krenzel and came down with the ball between two defenders for a 45-yard gain. That led to the decisive three-yard touchdown catch by tight end Ben Hartsock as the fourth-ranked Buckeyes (8-0, 3-0 in the Big Ten) won for the third straight time in always-rowdy Camp Randall Stadium.

Ohio State overcame two quick-strike scores by the Badgers (5-3, 0-3) and a 144-yard rushing performance by tailback Anthony Davis to keep alive its hopes for a Big Ten title and a spot in the BCS national championship game.

"We were calm throughout," Jenkins said, discussing that huge third-down conversion. "We needed one play to jump-start us, and I was there to make the catch.

"Even though I was double-covered a lot, we needed to take that shot."

The other "shot" OSU needed to take also paid huge

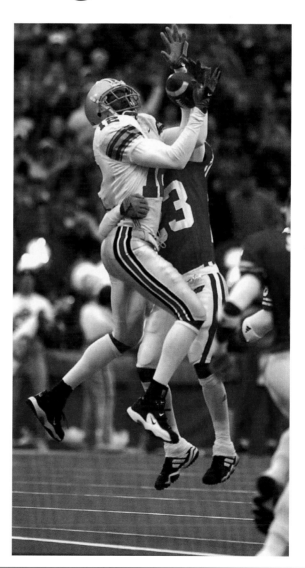

Opposite page:
Teammates congratulate Chris Gamble after he intercepted a pass to thwart a Wisconsin drive. *(Jason J. Molyet/Newspaper Network of Central Ohio/Mansfield News Journal)*

Left: OSU receiver Michael Jenkins hauls in a pass over Badger defender B.J. Tucker during Ohio State's winning drive. *(Jason J. Molyet/ Newspaper Network of Central Ohio/ Mansfield News Journal)*

dividends. With Wisconsin poised to answer the Buckeyes' go-ahead score, wide receiver Chris Gamble was summoned to play cornerback on third and 11 from the OSU 29. Jim Sorgi, who took over at quarterback when starter Brooks Bollinger suffered a concussion in the second quarter, immediately picked on Gamble by throwing a fade pass down the left side to freshman Jonathan Orr.

Orr already had scored on a 42-yard post pattern at the expense of freshman E.J. Underwood. But this time Gamble picked off the pass in the end zone on an effort reminiscent of his crucial goal-line

interception against Cincinnati.

"That's huge; you see how (Gamble) goes up for the ball," OSU coach Jim Tressel said of his two-way star, whose 48-yard catch in the first half led to a field goal. "It doesn't matter if he's the intended receiver or he's in coverage; you wish you could play him all the time."

Maurice "One and Done?" Clarett failed to score a touchdown for the first time this season, but the freshman tailback rushed for 133 yards on 30 carries and got the tough yards during crunch time, gaining 28 yards on six carries as the Buckeyes ran the last 4:29 off the clock.

Above: OSU defensive lineman Tim Anderson trips up Wisconsin quarterback Brooks Bollinger. *(Jason J. Molyet/Newspaper Network of Central Ohio/Mansfield News Journal)*

Right: OSU's Michael Doss holds on to Wisconsin's Matt Bernstein. *(Jason J. Molyet/Newspaper Network of Central Ohio/ Mansfield News Journal)*

Clarett wouldn't address the recent cover story in "ESPN the Magazine" that has him thinking of challenging an NFL rule prohibiting freshmen from entering the draft, but he was more than happy to talk about the victory as a character-builder.

"It was all about character today," Clarett said. "We showed a lot of discipline and poise. People were making plays when we needed them."

Ohio State needed only three plays to strike first. Clarett gained 25 yards to midfield, followed by a three-yard run by Chris Gamble on a reverse to set up the payoff — a 47-yard hookup between Krenzel and Jenkins (five catches, 114 yards). Cornerback B.J. Tucker missed a tackle when the ball arrived, allowing Jenkins to turn a short slant-in pass into a long TD just 1:30 into the game.

The Badgers tied it in the first quarter on a 41-yard sideline sprint by Davis, but OSU fired right back as a 48-yard floater from Krenzel to Gamble led to a 27-yard field goal by Mike Nugent with 2:48 left in the period. That put the Buckeyes back in front 10-7 and Nugent in the OSU

Far left: Michael Jenkins celebrates a first-quarter touchdown. *(Jason J. Molyet/ Newspaper Network of Central Ohio/ Mansfield News Journal)*

Left: Brandon Schnittker pushes away Badger defender Scott Starks. *(Jason J. Molyet/Newspaper Network of Central Ohio/Mansfield News Journal)*

record books with his 16th straight field goal.

Nugent made it 17 in a row, expanding OSU's lead to 13-7, on a 25-yard field goal early in the second quarter after Mike Doss recovered a botched snap from center. But Wisconsin kept battling, even after losing Bollinger following consecutive sacks by Cie Grant and Simon Fraser.

Two plays after Sorgi failed to hit Orr on a deep post pattern, the Badgers went back to the same play. This time it went for a 42-yard touchdown strike to Orr, putting Wisconsin in front 14-13 at the break.

Left: OSU running back Maurice Clarett carries Badger defender Broderick Williams. *(Jason J. Molyet/Newspaper Network of Central Ohio/Mansfield News Journal)*

Above: OSU quarterback Craig Krenzel is sacked in the first half by a gang of Badger defenders. *(Jason J. Molyet/Newspaper Network of Central Ohio/Mansfield News Journal)*

But the Buckeyes have made the necessary halftime adjustments all season, and this game was no different. They held the Badgers to 136 yards total offense in the second half and zero yards rushing in the fourth quarter.

"We were defeated by a very good football team today," UW coach Barry Alvarez said. "No one likes to lose, but I liked the way my guys competed. They just made a couple of more plays than we did."

Above: Coach Jim Tressel urges on his team. *(Jason J. Molyet/Newspaper Network of Central Ohio/Mansfield News Journal)*

Left: OSU tight end Ben Hartsock celebrates what turned out to be the winning touchdown. *(Jason J. Molyet/Newspaper Network of Central Ohio/Mansfield News Journal)*

#4 Ohio State vs Wisconsin
(Oct. 19, 2002 at Madison, Wis.)

Score by Quarters	1	2	3	4	Score	
Ohio State	10	3	0	6	19	Record: (8-0,3-0)
Wisconsin	7	7	0	0	14	Record: (5-3,0-3)

Buckeyes grind out 13-7 win over Penn State

By Jon Spencer
Newspaper Network of Central Ohio

COLUMBUS – Fans who think the 2002 Ohio State Buckeyes are a team of destiny or leading a charmed existence saw those beliefs reinforced in a gritty, 13-7 victory over Penn State.

The fourth-ranked Buckeyes (9-0, 4-0 in the Big Ten) overcame four turnovers, the absence of defensive sparkplug Cie Grant, the opening series loss of tailback sensation Maurice Clarett and the failure to score an offensive touchdown to remain in the national championship hunt.

It was OSU's fifth home win in as many tries over the Lions and coaching icon Joe Paterno since Penn State joined the Big Ten in 1993.

"I don't think you can say (we're) destined," quarterback Craig Krenzel said after throwing two interceptions and fumbling as he tried to lunge across the goal line on OSU's opening drive.

"It just shows what kind of team we are. We may be young, but we're a team with a lot of depth. We've been able to overcome adversity and find ways to win games."

The Buckeyes lost Clarett to a shoulder stinger

Left: Penn State's Matt Schmitt tries to bring down OSU linebacker A.J. Hawk after Hawk intercepted a tipped pass by Lion quarterback Zack Mills in the first quarter.
(Dave Polcyn/Newspaper Network of Central Ohio/Mansfield News Journal)

Right: Craig Krenzel fumbles on the Penn State one yard line in the first quarter. *(Christopher Crook/Newspaper Network of Central Ohio/Zanesville Times Recorder)*

on the first series after he went over 1,000 yards rushing for the season. Without him, OSU turned to its "other" phenom. Chris Gamble responded with a touchdown-saving tackle and game-winning touchdown.

As usual, Gamble ran with the first-teamers at flanker. The sophomore from Sunrise, Fla., also made his starting debut at cornerback, where he picked off the first pass thrown in his direction by quarterback Zack Mills and zig-zagged 40 yards to put OSU in front 10-7 two minutes into the third period.

The defense took it from there, holding the 18th-ranked Lions (5-3, 2-3) to 58 yards total offense in the second half. Mike Nugent added his second 37-yard field

Above: Michael Jenkins stretches for yardage between Penn State's Derek Wake and Richard Gardner after catching a pass in the first quarter. *(Dave Polcyn/Newspaper Network of Central Ohio/Mansfield News Journal)*

Right: PSU's Derek Wake reaches for Lydell Ross. *(Bill Sinden/Newspaper Network of Central Ohio/Marion Star)*

goal of the game for an insurance score, running his streak of three-point conversions to 19 straight.

"Chris is a great player, but he's also a smart player," OSU coach Jim Tressel said of Gamble. "There are a lot of talented players, but he has a feel for the game. You could line him up just about anywhere ... and he pays close attention to what is going on on the field."

He may have been the only Buckeye paying attention when cornerback Anwar Phillips scooped up Krenzel's goal-line fumble on the game's opening series and appeared headed for six points the other way. Gamble eventually shed the blocking of persistent corner Richard Gardner and brought down Phillips at the OSU 41.

That tackle loomed even larger two plays later when freshman linebacker A.J. Hawk — starting for the injured Grant — intercepted a pass deflected by OSU tackle Tim Anderson to kill that

Above, right: Maurice Clarett runs for 30 yards on his first carry of the game. He left with a shoulder injury soon after. *(Dave Polcyn/Newspaper Network of Central Ohio/Mansfield News Journal)*

Left: Penn State's Larry Johnson barely makes it into the end zone in the second quarter. *(Bill Sinden/Newspaper Network of Central Ohio/Marion Star)*

Right: Penn State quarterback Zack Mills is forced to throw out of bounds in the first quarter as Buckeye lineman Darrion Scott brings him down. *(Dave Polcyn/Newspaper Network of Central Ohio/Mansfield News Journal)*

Above: Mike Nugent kicks a second-quarter field goal out of the hold of punter Andy Groom. *(Christopher Crook/Newspaper Network of Central Ohio/Zanesville Times Recorder)*

Right: Chris Gamble slices through Penn State tacklers as he looks for the end zone after intercepting a pass in the third quarter. *(Kevin Graff/Newspaper Network of Central Ohio/Newark Advocate)*

Below: Michael Jenkins can't quite haul in a pass in the end zone as Richard Gardner defends. *(Kevin Graff/Newspaper Network of Central Ohio/Newark Advocate)*

scoring threat.

Penn State rebounded on its next possession to score on a five-yard option run by Larry Johnson. The senior tailback gained 40 yards, 35 on one carry, during that 80-yard drive. The rest of the afternoon he was held to 26 yards on 14 carries and the Lions mustered only 179 yards total offense.

"We didn't execute; our offense was ridiculous," said Johnson, who one week earlier had a school-record 257 yards rushing in a 49-0 rout of Northwestern. "Our defense played their hearts out. All we had to do was make one or two more blocks and it's a different ballgame."

Left: Chris Gamble returns an interception for a 40-yard touchdown in the third quarter.
(Christopher Crook/Newspaper Network of Central Ohio/Zanesville Times Recorder)

For the second year in a row, Mills was intercepted three times by the Buckeyes, with OSU converting the mistakes into 10 points.

Last year, Mills compensated by throwing for 280 yards and rushing for another 138 as the Lions rallied from 18 points down for a 29-27 victory. This time, he accounted for only seven yards on the ground and 98 through the air on 14 of 28 completions.

"The coaches got on us all week about Mills breaking the school record for total offense against

us last year," defensive end Will Smith said. "For him to do that as a freshman, we took that as a challenge."

Ohio State scored on 34 of 36 trips inside the red zone entering the game, but Krenzel fumbled at the goal line to ruin a 15-play march on the opening series and wide receiver Chris Vance fumbled at the PSU 15 in the second quarter to waste another scoring opportunity.

The Buckeyes wouldn't be deterred. It's a trait shared by teams of destiny.

"A lot of little things

hurt us, and that's a good (OSU) football team," Paterno said. "I think they are better defensively than they were last year. Obviously they didn't know as much about Mills last year as they do now.

"I think it was just a combination of them playing very well and we couldn't make a play."

#18 Penn State vs #4 Ohio State						
(Oct. 26, 2002 at Columbus, Ohio)						
Score by Quarters	1	2	3	4	Score	
Penn State	7	0	0	0	7	Record: (5-3,2-3)
Ohio State	0	3	10	0	13	Record: (9-0,4-0)

Above: Kenny Peterson and Simon Fraser celebrate a fourth-quarter sack of Zack Mills.
(Bill Sinden/Newspaper Network of Central Ohio/Marion Star)

Left: Ben Hartsock (88) and Buckeye teammates celebrate their victory.
(Kevin Graff/Newspaper Network of Central Ohio/Newark Advocate)

Buckeye defense spurs 34-3 pounding of Golden Gophers

By Jon Spencer
Newspaper Network of Central Ohio

COLUMBUS — You could have heard a pin — or, more fittingly, a flustered running back, harassed quarterback or penalty flag — drop.

Ohio State safety Donnie Nickey thought the Minnesota Golden Gophers might engage him in some trash talk after he questioned the suspect schedule they played en route to a 7-1 record.

But he didn't hear a peep.

In fact, the 104,897 in Ohio Stadium kept waiting for the supposedly high-powered Gophers to show some sign of life as fourth-ranked OSU held No. 23 Minnesota to 112 yards total offense — just seven in the second half — for a 34-3 victory.

The Buckeyes (10-0, 5-0 in the Big Ten) did it without tailback Maurice Clarett, whose left shoulder injury kept the freshman sensation watching the rout from the sidelines.

"What I said and what ended up in the Minnesota paper, I don't know understand why it was a big deal," said Nickey, who suggested earlier in the week that the Gophers hadn't played anyone the caliber of Ohio State.

"My coaches kind of got on me. 'Are you talking smack?' I thought it was an honest assessment, and I think we proved it."

The Gophers, ranked No. 1 in the Big Ten and sixth nationally in rushing, were rendered speechless after being held to 53 yards on 36 attempts. Terry Jackson II, the league's leading ground-gainer, mustered just 49

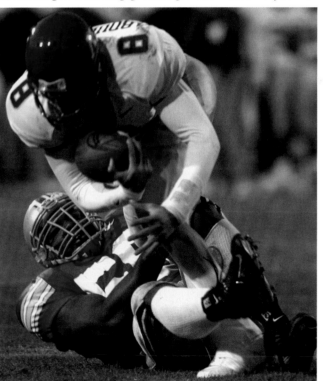

Opposite page:
Buckeye defenders swarm Minnesota's Terry Jackson II. *(James Miller/ Newspaper Network of Central Ohio/ Marion Star)*

Left: Ohio State's Darrion Scott hauls down Minnesota quarterback Asad Abdul-Khaliq in the second half. *(William P. Cannon/ Newspaper Network of Central Ohio/ Lancaster Eagle-Gazette)*

yards on 16 carries for Minnesota, whose longest gain from scrimmage was 11 yards.

"I didn't hear a word (from them)," Nickey said, with a wry grin. "I'm sure it would have been different if they had run it up on us."

There wasn't much chance of that happening. With Minnesota's running game stymied, the Big Ten's worst passing offense was in no condition to bail out the Gophers (7-2, 3-2). Quarterback Asad Abdul-Khaliq managed only 59 yards passing on 10 completions and was sacked four times.

So dominant were the Buckeyes that Minnesota was flagged four times for holding.

"We knew that Minnesota was in the top 10 in the nation in rushing and we didn't want them controlling the clock," safety Mike Doss said. "It was 11 guys working hard (on defense) and believing in themselves."

Ohio State has allowed only 10 points over the last 10 quarters and has shut out its last four opponents in the second half.

"Part of it is confidence and part of it is playing a Big Ten schedule," Nickey said, referring to the more conventional offenses the Buckeyes have seen in conference play after being fed a steady diet of "spread" attacks in the non-conference season.

"We're playing physical teams now and getting used to the pounding. It's just an attitude, knowing we have a

Opposite page: Michael Jenkins outruns the Minnesota defense on a 49-yard pass play in the second quarter. *(James Miller/Newspaper Network of Central Ohio/Marion Star)*

Left: Ohio State's Maurice Hall is forced out of bounds by Justin Isom after breaking a long run. *(Daniel Melograna/Newspaper Network of Central Ohio/Mansfield News Journal)*

Below: OSU quarterback Craig Krenzel is smothered by Gopher defenders. *(Daniel Melograna/ Newspaper Network of Central Ohio/ Mansfield News Journal)*

chance to do a lot of things as a team."

Nickey's blocked punt led to a late first-half field goal and provided momentum for another second-half pullaway by the Buckeyes. They outscored the Gophers 24-0 in the final two periods and have now outclassed the opposition 175-38 after intermission this season.

Apparently, Minnesota coach and OSU alum Glen Mason wasn't watching the same game as everyone else.

"If you look at today's score, I think it's somewhat misleading," Mason said. "To come into a setting like Ohio Stadium and perform the way we did,

Below: OSU's Chris Gamble knocks down a pass intended for Minnesota's Antoine Burns. *(William P. Cannon/ Newspaper Network of Central Ohio/ Lancaster Eagle-Gazette)*

Opposite page: Ohio State's Chris Vance hauls in a 30-yard touchdown pass behind Minnesota's Ukee Dozier in the third quarter. *(Daniel Melograna/Newspaper Network of Central Ohio/Mansfield News Journal)*

Above: OSU receiver Chris Vance celebrates the third-quarter touchdown catch. *(Daniel Melograna/Newspaper Network of Central Ohio/Mansfield News Journal)*

I think says a lot. The perception that we did not play good because we allowed 34 points, I don't think is true."

Mason obviously felt holding the Buckeyes to 322 yards was a moral victory. Still, tailbacks Lydell Ross (89 yards, 20 carries, two TDs) and Maurice Hall (93 yards, 14 carries, one TD) performed admirably in Clarett's absence, Mike Nugent kicked two more field goals and Chris Vance caught a 30-yard TD pass from quarterback Craig Krenzel on the day he found out his brother was murdered in their hometown of Fort Myers, Fla.

Above, right: Ohio State running back Lydell Ross scores the Buckeyes' first touchdown. *(Daniel Melograna/ Newspaper Network of Central Ohio/ Mansfield News Journal)*

Right: OSU quarterback Craig Krenzel looks downfield. *(Dante Smith/ Newspaper Network of Central Ohio/ Zanesville Times Recorder)*

Far right: OSU running back Lydell Ross fumbles in the first quarter, ending a Buckeye drive. *(William P. Cannon/Newspaper Network of Central Ohio/Lancaster Eagle- Gazette)*

"There are doubters out there, but I don't worry about them," Ross said about the skeptics who downgrade OSU's attack without Clarett. "We have other tailbacks who can step up and bring something to the table. If you put us in the game, we can do it."

#23 Minnesota vs #4 Ohio State						
(Nov. 2, 2002 at Columbus, Ohio)						
Score by Quarters	1	2	3	4	Score	
Minnesota	3	0	0	0	3	Record: (7-2,3-2)
Ohio State	0	10	17	7	34	Record: (10-0,5-0)

Above: Teammates congratulate Lydell Ross after his second touchdown of the game.
(Daniel Melograna/Newspaper Network of Central Ohio/Mansfield News Journal)

Left: Ohio State defenders Pat O'Neil (36), Fred Pagac Jr. (46), and Mike Kudla converge on Minnesota's Antoine Burns in the second half.
(James Miller/Newspaper Network of Central Ohio/Marion Star)

Buckeyes get heart-stopping victory vs. Boilermakers

By Jon Spencer
Newspaper Network of Central Ohio

WEST LAFAYETTE, Ind. — A battle-weary Craig Krenzel shuffled into the locker room, rolled his eyes heavenward and exhaled with a throaty "Whoa!"

Whoa, indeed.

Ohio State's thrilling yet chilling game of "Beat The Clock" stopped hearts but kept the pulse of a perfect football season thumping as the Buckeyes escaped Ross-Ade Stadium with a 10-6 victory.

With no timeouts remaining, OSU rushed its field goal unit onto the field for Mike Nugent's game-tying 22-yarder as time expired in the first half. The Buckeyes were racing the clock again when Krenzel delivered the game-winning 37-yard touchdown pass to Michael Jenkins with 1:36 remaining.

That Ohio State opted not to burn a timeout on that decisive fourth-and-one call simply added to the suspense.

"We called the play at the line of scrimmage," Krenzel said. "No one was thinking about our season hanging on one play."

So focused was tight end Ben Hartsock on the task at hand that he didn't realize the third-ranked Buckeyes

(11-0, 6-0 in the Big Ten) had no margin for error.

"It was fourth down, wasn't it?" Hartsock said, incredulously. "Looking back, that is the play of the year right now. Looking back, I'm glad we didn't (call

Opposite page: OSU's Cie Grant, Robert Reynolds and Mike Doss crunch Purdue's Joey Harris. *(Kevin Graff/Newspaper Network of Central Ohio/Newark Advocate)*

Left: Michael Jenkins pulls in the winning touchdown over Purdue's Antwaun Rogers in the fourth quarter. *(Michael Heinz/ Gannett News Service/Lafayette (Ind.) Journal and Courier)*

Right: OSU tight end Ben Hartsock is brought down by Purdue's Landon Johnson after catching a pass in the first quarter. *(Kevin Graff/ Newspaper Network of Central Ohio/ Newark Advocate)*

a timeout) because then maybe we start thinking, 'OK, this is it.'

"We just went out, called the play and it worked. If you do take a timeout there, you might seize up."

Krenzel had three options on the play. The first was Hartsock running an underneath pattern over the middle. Chris Gamble ran a 15-yard dig route down the right side and Jenkins adjusted his post route, turning outside toward the

left sideline when pressed by cornerback Antwaun Rogers.

"My read was if Ben was open to get him the ball for the first down," Krenzel said. "I couldn't hit him today to save my life. Thank God he wasn't open.

"I think they thought maybe we'd run the ball since it was fourth and one, so they went straight man-to-man, with no deep safety. They brought the blitz off the edge, but the line did a great job of picking it up and Mike ran a great route. He got a step on his man and I just got him the ball."

The late-game heroics masked an otherwise awful performance by the Ohio State offense. Krenzel fumbled twice (both recovered by the Buckeyes), and his first-quarter interception on a deflected pass led to a 21-yard

field goal and 3-0 lead by the Boilermakers.

Purdue (4-6, 2-4) outgained Ohio State 341-267 in total yardage, holding the Buckeyes to 101 yards in the second half. The running game went nowhere, especially after freshman tailback Maurice Clarett (52 yards, 14 carries) aggravated his left shoulder stinger and left the game for good in the third period.

It was Ohio State's lowest scoring output since a 13-6 loss at UCLA in last season's second game. The last time the Buckeyes scored as few as 10 points in a winning cause was in 1987, when they won by the identical score at Illinois.

"This may or may not be hard to believe, but the game

Below, left: Ohio State's Dustin Fox makes an interception in the back of the end zone in the first quarter. *(Kevin Graff/Newspaper Network of Central Ohio/Newark Advocate)*

Below, right: Chris Gamble turns upfield after catching a pass. Purdue's Ralph Turner prepares to tackle him. *(Kevin Graff/Newspaper Network of Central Ohio/Newark Advocate)*

played out exactly as we had hoped," Purdue coach Joe Tiller said. "Ohio State has the best defense in the Big Ten and one of the best in the nation, so we just wanted to be in position to win the game in the fourth quarter.

"We just didn't get the key stop on a fourth-down play and then didn't operate the two-minute offense. Those two things were the deciding factor in the game."

A 58-yard pass from relief quarterback Brandon Kirsch to Ray Williams led to a 32-yard field goal by Berin Lacevic, giving Purdue a 6-3 lead with 7:50 to play. Those were the first second-half points surrendered by the Buckeyes in five games.

But with the clock starting to work against OSU, Purdue punter Brent Slaton made the critical mistake of outkicking his coverage. Chris Gamble returned Slaton's 57-yard punt 22 yards to set up the Buckeyes' winning TD drive. The two-way starter

then sealed Purdue's fate by intercepting a deep pass from starting quarterback Kyle Orton at the OSU 11 with 45 seconds remaining.

"Our guys wouldn't fold; they kept slugging away," Ohio State coach Jim Tressel said. "We always talk about if you keep banging away, something good is going to happen."

Asked how he would rate the dramatic victory, Tressel deadpanned, "It's the best win of the day."

Below, left: Michael Jenkins scoops up the ball after he blocked a Purdue punt in the third quarter. *(Kevin Graff/ Newspaper Network of Central Ohio/Newark Advocate)*

Below, right: Mike Doss celebrates after Mike Nugent's field goal ended the first half. *(Kevin Graff/Gannett News Service/Newark Advocate)*

#3 Ohio State vs Purdue
(Nov. 9, 2002 at West Lafayette, Ind.)

Score by Quarters	1	2	3	4	Score	
Ohio State	0	3	0	7	10	Record: (11-0,6-0)
Purdue	3	0	0	3	6	Record: (4-6,2-4)

Tressel didn't exactly roll dice on game-winning Purdue play

By Jon Spencer
Newspaper Network of Central Ohio

WEST LAFAYETTE, Ind. — Ohio State football coach Jim Tressel isn't considered a buttoned-up guy just because he wears collared shirts with his gameday sweater vest and tie.

In the 10-6 win at Purdue, Tressel came away looking like a high-stakes gambler when Craig Krenzel threw a 37-yard touchdown pass to Michael Jenkins on fourth and one with 1:36 remaining. But Krenzel's first option, or "read," on that play was a simple, high-percentage pass over the middle to tight end Ben Hartsock for the first down.

When Hartsock got "mangled" — Jenkins' description — Krenzel went deep to his junior split end, making Tressel look like a go-for-broke wheeler-dealer throwing caution to the wind (which, incidentally, the Buckeyes were marching into on their game-winning drive).

True to his conservative nature, Tressel was ready to put OSU's perfect season on the perfect right foot of kicker Mike Nugent by booting a game-tying field goal and taking his chances in overtime.

"As you think about scenarios in decision-making, you always say, 'Would overtime be a good thing for us?' " Tressel said. "The way we were playing defense and the

way we have kicked field goals, it would not have been a bad thing."

Tressel's biggest gamble on that play was electing not to use one of two remaining timeouts to discuss the Buckeyes' options. Especially with a perfect season and Big Ten championship riding on that one play.

Left: Michael Jenkins, right, gets a hug from lineman Shane Olivea after catching the winning touchdown. *(Kevin Graff/ Newspaper Network of Central Ohio/ Newark Advocate)*

"Sometimes if you give us coaches a chance to think, we foul things up," Tressel said, smiling. "I'm not sure we would have called anything different.

"It was a route that had all the components. We had a quick throw or a dump-off for a first down and also the (option was there for) big-play potential. So I don't think we would have done anything different."

Tressel pointed out that Jenkins' heroics — he adjusted his post route outside when pressed inside by cornerback Antwaun Rogers — wouldn't have been possible if Krenzel hadn't reacted just as well under pressure.

"The crucial thing Craig did was step up (in the pocket) and slide forward," Tressel said. "That gave Michael that extra time to get separation (from Rogers)."

It was not as easy a throw as Krenzel made it look. A stiff wind was blowing in the Buckeyes' faces.

"The wind was tough," Tressel said. "The one thing Craig does is step up and throw a tight spiral. There's not as much surface of the ball getting affected (by wind) when he throws it as maybe some people.

Left: OSU quarterback Craig Krenzel breaks free of tacklers during a second-quarter run. *(Kevin Graff/Newspaper Network of Central Ohio/Newark Advocate)*

"He threw a bomb, but it was only 37 yards. It wasn't like he had to throw it 70. He had good form when he threw it, and when you cut it through the wind with a tight spiral, you have a chance of not being affected."

Until his game-winning hook-up with Jenkins, Krenzel wasn't having one of his more memorable afternoons. He posted decent passing numbers (13 of 20, 173 yards), but he also committed two of OSU's three fumbles — all of which the Buckeyes recovered — and threw an interception that led to a Purdue field goal.

He almost single-handedly cost the Buckeyes a shot at putting points on the board when he got tackled at the five on a quarterback draw with 12 seconds left in the first half and no timeouts remaining. Nugent rushed onto the field and made a 22-yard field goal as time expired.

"We wanted it to be that we throw for a touchdown or throw it out of bounds, but Craig felt he could make it (to the end zone by running)," Tressel said. "He

saw the Red Sea part there. That's not what we wanted, but you've got to like a guy who believes in himself, especially when we end up with a field goal."

Below: Linebacker Matt Wilhelm celebrates with fans after the game.
(Kevin Graff/Newspaper Network of Central Ohio/Newark Advocate)

Calm Buckeyes win another nail-biter — 23-16 at Illinois

By Jon Spencer
Newspaper Network of Central Ohio

CHAMPAIGN, Ill. — When Illinois kicked the game-tying field goal as time expired in regulation, Ohio State knew it had the Illini right where it wanted them.

Seriously.

With a perfect season imperiled, the situation looked anything but dire in the faces of some of the Buckeyes before they went back on the field for the first overtime in school history.

"I've been in some overtime games, but I'm not sure any of those kids have," coach Jim Tressel said. "When we were standing there before the (OT) toss, Donnie Nickey and Mike Doss were commenting on how much fun it was. They were saying 'Hey, this is what it's all about.' "

How about you, coach? Were you having fun?

"Absolutely," Tressel said.

The best part was retracing the extra steps that led to a 23-16 victory, making Ohio State 12-0 for the first time and putting the Buckeyes (7-0 in the Big Ten) within one victory — over archrival Michigan at home — from earning a share of the league title with Iowa. A win and OSU will play for the national championship in the Jan. 3 Fiesta Bowl.

Illinois won the OT toss and elected to play

Left: Dejected Illinois quarterback John Beutjer (7) walks off the field as Ohio State celebrates its overtime victory.
(James Miller/Newspaper Network of Central Ohio/Marion Star)

Right: Illini defender Jamie Hanton grabs the facemask of OSU quarterback Craig Krenzel in overtime.
(James Miller/Newspaper Network of Central Ohio/Marion Star)

defense first, with the ball placed at the Illini 25. On third and 10, quarterback Craig Krenzel scrambled from the pocket on a pass play and picked up 14 yards to the 11.

Two plays later, tailback Maurice Hall followed the blocking of mammoth left guard Adrien Clarke into the end zone for what proved to be the decisive, eight-yard score, putting an even bigger grin on Michael Jenkins' face than he was wearing before the drive began.

"I would say we were calm on the sidelines," said Jenkins, who had six catches for 147 yards and scored in the third quarter on a 50-yard reception. "It felt like the beginning of the game. I was smiling because I knew we were going to score."

But OSU's victory wasn't secure until two end-zone passes by Illini quarterback Jon Beutjer (27 of 45, 305 yards) were

called incomplete. On second and eight from the nine, Aaron Moorehead was ruled out of bounds on his attempted catch in the right corner of the end zone.

Cornerback Dustin Fox didn't give Moorehead room to come down inbounds. In the NFL, his catch would have been ruled a TD, but receivers receive no such benefit on the collegiate level.

On third down, Beutjer tested corner Chris Gamble in the left corner of the end zone, but the official ruled wide receiver Walter Young was bobbling the ball on his way out of bounds.

Beutjer's last-gasp pass never got beyond the line of scrimmage as tackle Tim Anderson batted it down with his left forearm.

Below, right: OSU linebackers Cie Grant and Matt Wilhelm bring down Illinois' Antoineo Harris. *(James Miller/Newspaper Network of Central Ohio/Marion Star)*

Below: Illini quarterback Jon Beutjer tries to throw over OSU defensive lineman Tim Anderson. *(James Miller/Newspaper Network of Central Ohio/Marion Star)*

of the end zone. On television replays, he appeared to be in the end zone. He was marked out at the one, however, and after three straight illegal procedure penalties, the Buckeyes settled for a field goal.

The win was the Buckeyes' sixth second-half comeback of the season and gives them five victories on the road by a total of 31 points.

"We're definitely toeing the line," tight end Ben Hartsock said of OSU's tightrope walks. "It's not something I'm really excited about. I don't really want to get into those situations. I don't think anybody wants to.

"It makes for an ESPN Classic game, but it also makes for lesser years on your life."

Mike Nugent's streak of 24 consecutive field goals came to an end on a 37-yard attempt into a stiff wind in the second quarter. But without freshman tailback Maurice Clarett (shoulder stinger), OSU still rode Nugent's right leg to a 6-3 halftime lead before surrendering its first second-half touchdown in six games.

Young's 19-yard catch over Fox put the Illini in front 10-6 in the third quarter. The Buckeyes answered immediately on Krenzel's 50-yard TD strike

Left: Lydell Ross breaks loose in the first quarter.
(James Miller/Newspaper Network of Central Ohio/Marion Star)

Below: Buckeye safety Mike Doss just misses an interception in front of Illini receiver Greg Lewis.
(James Miller/Newspaper Network of Central Ohio/Marion Star)

Neither end-zone call sat well with the Illini faithful, who lustily booed Ohio State and chanted "Over-rated!" at the top of their lungs as the Buckeyes headed for their locker room.

"I'd like to have instant replay all the time," Illini coach Ron Turner said after his team fell to 4-7 (3-4 in the Big Ten) and out of bowl contention. "It's a crying shame for those kids, if the game was decided by the officials. Anyone who is against instant replay should walk into (our) locker room and see the look in those players' eyes."

What Turner failed to mention is that instant replay probably would have given the Buckeyes a win in regulation. During a first-quarter drive, Krenzel stretched for the corner down the left side to Jenkins, but John Gockman booted a 47-yard field goal for Illinois to forge a 13-13 tie heading into the final period.

Nugent's third field goal, a 37-yarder, put Ohio State back in front until Beutjer completed four passes in the final 1:04 to set up Gockman's game-tying 48-yard field goal as the clock ran out.

Suddenly, a long season got even longer for the Buckeyes. But afterwards they were feeling no pain.

"Overtime meant more plays in what was already a close, physical game," Tressel said. "Game No. 13 (against Michigan) is coming up, so our energy level better be fine."

#2 Ohio State vs Illinois
(Nov. 16, 2002 at Champaign, Ill.)

Score by Quarters	1	2	3	4	OT	Score	
Ohio State	6	0	7	3	7	23	Record: (12-0,7-0)
Illinois	0	3	10	3	0	16	Record: (4-7,3-4)

Right: OSU running back Maurice Hall falls into the end zone on an eight-yard touchdown run in overtime.
(James Miller/Newspaper Network of Central Ohio/Marion Star)

They don't get much credit, but Buckeye run not all luck

By Jon Spencer
Newspaper Network of Central Ohio

As the victories mount, so do the non-believers in second-ranked and unbeaten Ohio State.

The parade of cynics stretches from coast to coast, grand-marshaled by ESPN analysts Mark May and Trev Alberts. It's May who insists the escape artists in scarlet and gray would go 0-4 against the other teams ranked in the top five, despite having already manhandled No. 4 Washington State once this season. Alberts claims the Buckeyes would be a 14-point underdog to fifth-ranked Iowa.

Outside of ex-Buckeye Kirk Herbstreit, the duo has gotten few if any arguments from their colleagues at the "da-da-da, da-da-da" network.

Joining Alberts and May on a parade float could be Chicago Sun-Times columnist Jay Mariotti. He was underwhelmed by OSU from his view in the press box during the 23-16 overtime win at Illinois, calling the Buckeyes "undeserving" and "byte-sized" (an obvious slap at the computer geeks who manipulate the BCS rankings).

He figures the Buckeyes will get "shellacked" by Miami in their battle for the national championship and, as a proud Midwesterner, fears "complete humiliation."

"The Buckeyes are living on borrowed time," Mariotti wrote in his Sunday column, "doomed to be a flop in the Fiesta Bowl."

It's nothing Ohio State hasn't heard a thousand times before, even close to home.

"We're 12-0," said middle linebacker Matt Wilhelm, practically snarling. "Who cares (how we win)?"

The believers suggest if Ohio State were truly leading a charmed existence, it wouldn't have won the Illinois game on something as ordinary as an eight-yard run up the middle by tailback Maurice Hall.

The decisive score would have come on the second play of OT when Chris Vance dropped a 25-yard touchdown pass as he was approaching the end zone. A reception there would have really been something, seeing as how the throw wasn't intended for Vance.

"I was trying to hit Michael (Jenkins) across the middle at his knees," quarterback Craig Krenzel said sheepishly, "but the ball fluttered."

The non-believers feel they have plenty of ammo to back their contention that OSU has been ridiculously blessed all season.

How about Michael Jenkins losing the ball in the lights, never seeing it until it "fell into my hands" for a 50-yard TD pass against the Illini? How about Cincinnati receivers dropping two last-minute passes in the end zone?

How do the Buckeyes recover all three of their fumbles in the 10-6 squeaker over Purdue? Or keep winning without Maurice Clarett? Or lose Darrion Scott to a groin injury only to see his replacement, David Thompson, get credited with three sacks against Illinois? Or make due despite a variety of injuries on the offensive line? Or stay perfect despite being outgained each of the last two weeks?

"We just stick together; we're a team out there," Jenkins said. "We never give in or point the finger at anybody. We just keep fighting and find a way to win."

The Buckeyes obviously buy into the family values Tressel has extolled since his first day on the job.

"It goes back to the intangibles this team has — the respect guys have, the friendships and relationships that have developed," tight end Ben Hartsock said. "It's hard to translate that into X's and O's, but those small things can really make things bounce your way."

Most of them anyway.

If the Buckeyes were getting all the breaks, the officials wouldn't have blown the call on a Krenzel TD run in the first quarter at Illinois. The ball was placed at the one and three straight motion penalties forced Ohio State to settle for a field goal.

And Lady Luck wouldn't have been in a hot dog line when Krenzel overthrew a wide-open Chris Gamble on a long pass down the right sideline. She also wouldn't have greased the football as Krenzel was diving in for a score on the opening drive against Penn State.

There's obviously more at work here than good fortune. Perhaps it's all mere payback for last season, when 7-5 Ohio State lost four games by a total of 15 points.

"Nobody said it was going to be easy playing on the road to win a Big Ten championship," Jenkins said. "We just stuck together and played 60 minutes — 65 minutes (against Illinois) — and were able to pull it out."

That's happened a lot this season — six second-half comebacks, three fourth-quarter rallies, five road wins by a total of 31 points.

Hence all the talk about Ohio State being the poster boy for parity. The Buckeyes are just good enough to survive from week to week. Excuse the mixed metaphors, but each time they teeter on the brink of disaster, they wiggle off the hook.

"We're a well-coached team," Wilhelm said, "that in crunch time is making plays."

Opposite page:
Ohio State's Bobby Carpenter and Chris Conwell greet jubilant and relieved fans after the Illinois win. *(James Miller/Newspaper Network of Central Ohio/Marion Star)*

Jenkins does talking with game-turning plays

By Jon Spencer
Newspaper Network of Central Ohio

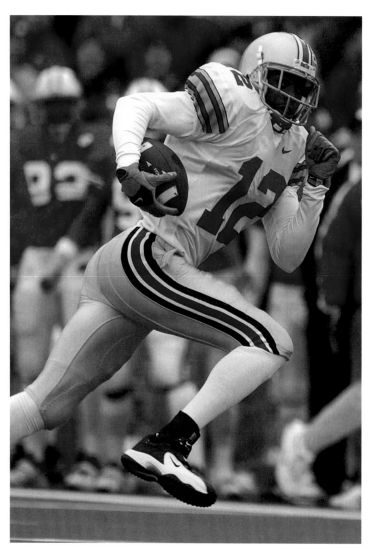

Right: Michael Jenkins sprints for a touchdown against Wisconsin. *(Jason J. Molyet/Newspaper Network of Central Ohio/Mansfield News Journal)*

COLUMBUS — Ohio State tight end Ben Hartsock is jealous. The 6-foot-4 junior is strong enough to mash linebackers, reliable enough to throw to in clutch situations and agile enough to make one-handed stabs.

Doesn't matter. He wants to be like Mike.

"If you throw it anywhere in his area, he's going to come up with the big play," Hartsock said of OSU split end Michael Jenkins. "To have a guy that tall and that athletic, I couldn't imagine having that kind of talent."

Hartsock isn't the only one who looks up to the 6-5 Jenkins. Michael Hall, a 5-10 cornerback for Illinois, spent last week's game craning his neck as Jenkins went over and around him for 147 yards in receptions in the Buckeyes' 23-16 overtime victory.

Jenkins caught six passes, reaching over Hall for a 50-yard touchdown catch on a ball he originally lost in the lights. It was reminiscent of the 37-yard grab he made on fourth down to beat Purdue 10-6 the week before.

With freshman tailback Maurice Clarett sidelined for most of the past month with a shoulder stinger, Jenkins has stepped up like an All-American for the Buckeyes. He's had more than 100 yards in receptions in three of the last six games and enters the Michigan game needing 20 yards to top 1,000 for the season.

Jenkins has caught 53 passes — 14 more than wideouts Chris Gamble and Chris Vance combined — and is tied with Lydell Ross for second on the team with six touchdowns. The junior from Tampa also averages 18.5 yards per catch, one of the best figures in the Big Ten.

"He's one of those guys that you don't even know is there because he's working," coach Jim Tressel said. "You love those kind of guys. Some guys you know they're there because they wear you out, they want you to know they're there. Mike is just a steady guy and a big-play guy."

Jenkins didn't mimic Terrell Owens and pull a Sharpie out of his sock after catching the dramatic game-winner on fourth down in the final two minutes against Purdue. Nor did he posture after catching a 47-yard TD pass against Wisconsin or preen after going high to make the 45-yard grab that led to the winning score against the Badgers.

Showboating is not his style.

"That's just been my mentality all along," Jenkins said. "Growing up I was real shy and didn't say much at all. It just stayed with me.

"I'm more of a quiet, laid-back guy who gets things done and leads by example. You can celebrate after the game."

Only once can Jenkins remember breaking out of character. It happened in high school after scoring a touchdown.

"I started dancing at the 50 and got flagged for it," he said, smiling. "I'm not sure why I did it. It came out somehow, but it was fun."

Jenkins has since traded in his dancing shoes for track spikes. He competed with the Ohio State track team this past winter and spring, running the 200 and 400 dashes and participating on sprint relays.

Already blessed with the height pro scouts drool over, Jenkins wanted to improve his footwork.

"I think I have decent speed," he said. "My long legs don't move as fast as little, quick legs that make players look like they're running faster. But I think I can get downfield and get open like other guys."

Jenkins has caught passes in 24 consecutive games. Michigan is one of only two teams to hold him to one catch in that stretch, limiting him to a 14-yard reception in last year's 26-20 win over the Wolverines.

"I've never demanded the football," said Jenkins, making him no Keyshawn Johnson in that regard. "We know if we get open, (Craig Krenzel) is going to find us because he does a great job of looking at all of his reads."

13-9 win over Michigan caps improbable 13-0 season

By Jon Spencer
Newspaper Network of Central Ohio

COLUMBUS — With four minutes remaining, freshman tailback Maurice Clarett sidled up to Ohio State coach Jim Tressel and said, "Man, why does the clock move so slow when we're winning?"

By now, Clarett should know the answer. He's been around long enough to know these nerve-wracking Buckeyes milk every ounce of drama out of every dwindling second.

They are the most exasperating, most exhilarating team around. They are also unbeaten Big Ten co-champions, headed for the Jan. 3 Fiesta Bowl for a crack at the national title after rallying to beat Michigan 14-9 before a raucous, record Ohio Stadium crowd of 105,539.

Maurice Hall scored the game-winning, three-yard touchdown with 4:55 to play on an option pitch the Buckeyes hadn't run all season. That gave Michigan time to mount two serious scoring threats, but both ended in turnovers as OSU won its second straight in this storied series for the first time since 1981-82.

It was Ohio State's seventh second-half

Opposite page: OSU running back Maurice Hall goes in for the winning score in the fourth quarter. *(Dante Smith/ Newspaper Network of Central Ohio/ Zanesville Times Recorder)*

Left: Fans try in vain to tear down the south goalposts after the game. *(Jason J. Molyet/Newspaper Network of Central Ohio/Mansfield News Journal)*

comeback and fourth rally in the fourth quarter. The second-ranked Buckeyes improved to 13-0 (8-0 in the Big Ten), winning for the third straight week — and sixth time this season — by seven points or less.

"The option pitch is something that had always been part of our package and it became an active part this week," Tressel said after accepting an invitation to the Bowl Championship Series title game from Fiesta Bowl officials.

"(Michigan does) a great job on goal-line defense, and we felt we had to do something to block one more guy. That's what the option is. You don't have to block a guy. You pitch off of him."

Many in the Horseshoe wondered if

Tressel had lost his mind when he took Clarett out and replaced him with Hall for that second-and-goal play. In his most significant action in five weeks, Clarett ignored the pain in his left shoulder and rushed for 119 yards on 20 carries.

He scored OSU's first touchdown on a two-yard run in the first quarter and also caught a 26-yard throwback

Below, left: A drummer grimaces during "Script Ohio" before the game. *(Dave Polcyn/Newspaper Network of Central Ohio/Mansfield News Journal)*

Below, right: Michigan's Braylon Edwards catches a touchdown over Ohio State's Chris Gamble in the second quarter. The score was called back on a pass interference penalty on Edwards. *(Kevin Graff/Newspaper Network of Central Ohio/Newark Advocate)*

pass down the left sideline that put the ball on the Michigan six on the decisive drive.

That, like the subsequent option run, was a new wrinkle in the attack, the kind of play you save all season for your archrival.

On the previous play, Tressel eschewed a 50-yard field goal attempt by Mike Nugent with the wind at his back, and went for it on fourth-and-one from the Michigan 33. Quarterback Craig Krenzel picked up the necessary yard on a sneak to keep the winning drive alive.

"For one thing, we needed less than a yard," Tressel said, explaining his decision, "and, two, Craig Krenzel would have killed me. He's such a competitor that he would have gone haywire if we hadn't gone for it on fourth down."

Ohio State's amazing run of good fortune continued against the ninth-ranked Wolverines (9-3, 6-2).

Destiny's team didn't bat an eye when the official first signaled TD on a 19-yard catch by Braylon Edwards in the second quarter before throwing a flag and calling offensive pass interference on Edwards instead.

As a result, the Wolverines were forced to settle for a third Adam Finley field goal and 9-7 lead at halftime.

If OSU isn't charmed, how did almost forgotten fullback Brandon Schnittker step in front of a pass

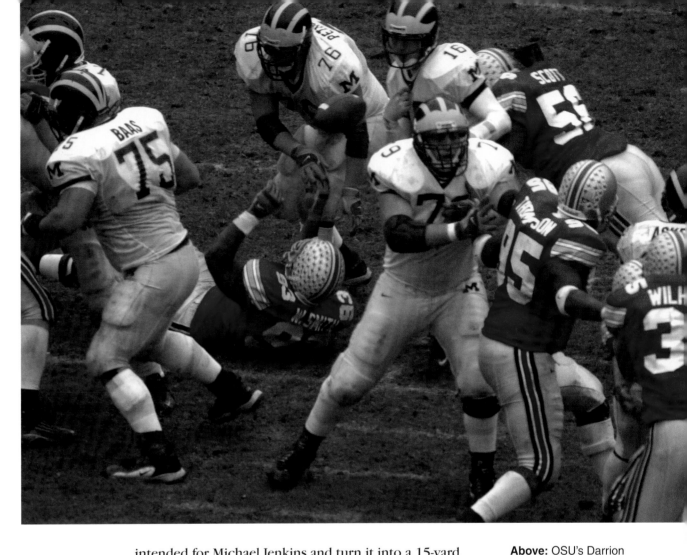

intended for Michael Jenkins and turn it into a 15-yard gain on the first play of the winning march?

"I just kind of instinctively reached up and grabbed it," Schnittker said of his catch over the middle. "I wasn't sure, but if it was for me and I didn't reach up, I'd feel worse, and if it was for me I grabbed it and ran for 15 yards. For whatever reason, it worked for us."

After allowing three field goals on drives of 12, 16 and 19 plays in the first half, the Buckeyes held Michigan to

Above: OSU's Darrion Scott hits Michigan quarterback John Navarre, causing a fumble late in the fourth quarter.
(Jason J. Molyet/Newspaper Network of Central Ohio/Mansfield News Journal)

157 yards and no points over the final two periods. It was the sixth time in the last seven weeks OSU hasn't allowed a TD after halftime, a stretch in which the opposition has scored just 13 second-half points.

Remarkably, the Buckeyes made their only third-down conversion on eight attempts with 12:56 left in the game. Michigan had twice as many first downs (26-13) and held the ball nearly 10 minutes more than Ohio State, which ranked second in the Big Ten in time of possession.

"From a statistical standpoint, we outplayed them," Michigan coach Lloyd Carr said, "but Ohio State did what it had to do to win the game."

Will Smith recovered a fumble by Michigan quarterback John Navarre at the OSU 36 after a sack by

Below, left:
Quarterback Craig Krenzel looks for a receiver after being flushed from the pocket by Michigan defenders.
(Dave Polcyn/Newspaper Network of Central Ohio/Mansfield News Journal)

Below, right: Buckeye Will Smith celebrates a first-half sack.
(Jason J. Molyet/Newspaper Network of Central Ohio/Mansfield News Journal)

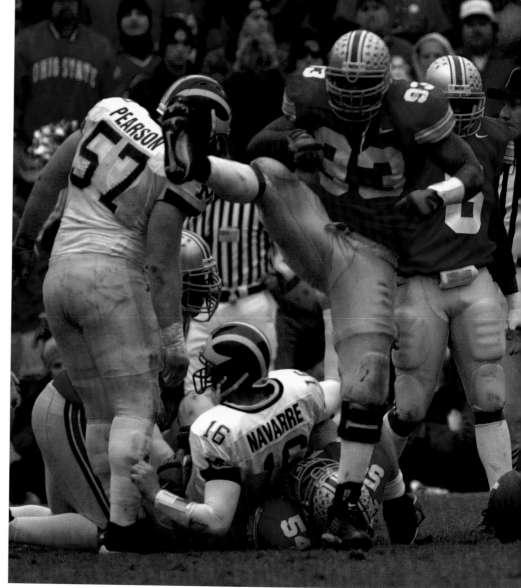

linemate Darrion Scott with 2:02 remaining and nickel back Will Allen intercepted a last-gasp 21-yard pass by Navarre at the OSU three as time expired.

"God has smiled down on us a few times," Schnittker said. "Some miraculous things have happened. It's great; I can't really describe the feeling right now."

Left: Maurice Clarett pushes past Michigan's Cato June for a first-quarter touchdown. *(Kevin Graff/ Newspaper Network of Central Ohio/Newark Advocate)*

Below: Buckeye Will Smith hits Michigan quarterback John Navarre as he releases a pass. *(Jason J. Molyet/ Newspaper Network of Central Ohio/Mansfield News Journal)*

#9 Michigan vs #2 Ohio State
(Nov. 23, 2002 at Columbus, Ohio)

Score by Quarters	1	2	3	4	Score	
Michigan	3	6	0	0	9	Record: (9-3,6-2)
Ohio State	7	0	0	7	14	Record: (13-0,8-0)

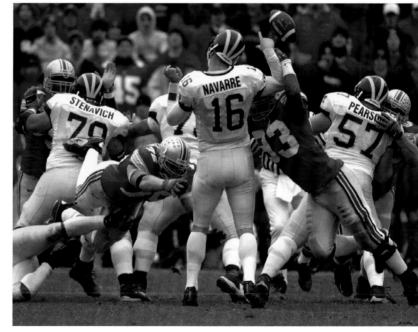

Above, left: Craig Krenzel hooks up with Maurice Clarett for a 26-yard gain on Ohio State's game-winning drive. *(Dante Smith/Newspaper Network of Central Ohio/Zanesville Times Recorder)*

Above, right: Maurice Clarett makes a catch at the Michigan six yard line during the winning drive. *(Dave Polcyn/Newspaper Network of Central Ohio/Mansfield News Journal)*

Right: OSU fans celebrate the go-ahead touchdown in the fourth quarter. *(Dave Polcyn/Newspaper Network of Central Ohio/Mansfield News Journal)*

'Scrappy' Buckeyes won on guts, not statistics

By Jon Spencer
Newspaper Network of Central Ohio

COLUMBUS — It's not every day you hear burly carnivores being asked if they like tortilla chips.

But that's exactly what happened in the postgame media questioning after Ohio State beat Michigan.

My guess is this silly query had something to do with Tostitos being the hosts in Tempe, Ariz. of the Fiesta Bowl-bound Buckeyes. (Darn, why didn't I think of that?)

A Wolf Blitzer wannabe dug up the fact that OSU coach Jim Tressel was a sports writer in college and asked him what headline he would put on the victory over Michigan.

"I suppose Ohio State 14, Michigan 9," Tressel said dryly. "Headline writers are overrated."

Cynics will scoff and say those headline writers have something in common with these Buckeyes after they continued to confound if not convince the experts.

How did they clinch a share of the Big Ten title and a national championship berth by converting only one third down against the Wolverines, and waiting more than three quarters to do so?

How did they repeatedly allow Michigan to convert on third-and-long and yet survive scoring drives of 12, 16 and 19 plays?

How did they hold the ball for only 25 of a possible 60 minutes, gain half as many first downs as Michigan, run 41 less plays and still win with so much at stake?

How did they run the table in the longest season in OSU history by scoring no more than two touchdowns in their last three games and in five of their last six?

"We've got a scrappy, tough, talented, smart bunch of folks that want to achieve," Tressel said.

Funny, "scrappy" used to be one of predecessor John Cooper's favorite adjectives. But these clearly are not Cooper's Buckeyes (even if he did recruit most of them).

Cooper's troops saw unbeaten seasons and national championship bids ruined three times by Michigan in the 1990s. That decade began with a rare option call by Cooper backfiring and paving the way to a last-second win by the Wolverines.

Ironically, a never-used option play produced the

Above: Maurice Clarett tells fans where he thinks the Buckeyes rank after the game. *(Dave Polcyn/ Newspaper Network of Central Ohio/ Mansfield News Journal)*

winning three-yard TD run by Maurice Hall vs. Michigan.

"The only thing we do with history is try to learn from it," said Tressel, who in two years has already beaten Michigan as many times as Cooper did in 13.

Tressel, the first OSU coach to beat Michigan in his first two tries since Francis Schmidt won four straight (1934-37), seems to possess the Midas touch Cooper never had except when he was ringing the doorbell at a recruit's home.

"The difference is belief," defensive tackle Tim Anderson said. "Our coaches do an incredible job of instilling confidence in us. They do a good job of keeping our heads up.

"The great thing when the defense comes off the field, having given up some points, coach Tressel is the first one on the field telling us it's all right; we'd get it back. We all believe in each other."

Something, however, tells me ESPN analyst Mike Gottfried isn't going to change his opinion of the Buckeyes based on what he saw — or didn't see — from the offense against the Wolverines.

When I asked the Crestline, Ohio, native last week to handicap a Fiesta Bowl showdown between the Buckeyes and defending national champion Miami, Gottfried forecast a meteorological nightmare. He basically said the Hurricanes would engulf an overmatched offensive line with the force of a tidal wave.

"Ohio State's defense and special teams can play with (Miami), but I think their offense will fall short," said Gottfried, who will work the title game for ESPN Radio. "Miami's front four on defense will handle Ohio State's front line, and (the Hurricanes) have so much skill, they'll just blanket those Ohio State receivers.

"They've got to be in a close game to have any chance to win a national championship. It changes a little bit with (Maurice) Clarett in there, but they still don't throw the ball well enough."

But like anybody who applauds the underdog, Gottfried can appreciate what Tressel and his scrappy Buckeyes have accomplished.

"I think (quarterback) Craig Krenzel has done what they need him to do," Gottfried said. "Really, they all have."

If this were the Division I-AA playoffs, it would be on to the finals again for Tressel, who won four I-AA titles and played in the title game six times in 15 years at Youngstown State.

"This seemed like a (semifinal) game," Tressel said. "I've been in six of those games and you knew if you won them you had a chance to stand at the top of the mountain if you did what you needed to do."

Are there any mountains in Tempe?

LUCKY 13

• Ohio State is 13-0 for the first time in school history.

• Tailback Maurice Clarett wears No. 13. He is the leading rusher and OSU freshman record-holder for rushing yards in a season (1,190), touchdowns (16), points scored (96) and 100-yard rushing games (seven)

• Kicker Mike Nugent, a Groza Award finalist, wears No. 85, which added together, equals 13

• Jim Tressel is 13-3 in Big Ten games as Ohio State head coach

• Michigan was the last home game for 13 OSU seniors

Left: Cie Grant holds up an inflatable Tostitos bag with coach Jim Tressel and Drew Carter in the background. *(Jason J. Molyet/Newspaper Network of Central Ohio/Mansfield News Journal)*

Buckeye fans take over Tempe

By Jay Hansen
Newspaper Network of Central Ohio

PHOENIX — They are everywhere. There is no escape.

"This town's totally Buckeye," said Dr. Chuck Cook, of Lancaster. "Every hotel that I've gone to, Ohio State has taken over."

It's not just the hotels. On the streets, in the restaurants and just about anywhere else you can think of, Buckeye fans have taken over, far outnumbering Miami football fans and painting the Valley of the Sun scarlet and gray. Brutus Buckeye could probably get elected mayor of Phoenix at this point.

"I didn't think there would be as many Ohio State fans here as there are, but they are all over the place," said Kathy Motycka, of Van Wert. "It feels more like Columbus than it does Tempe here."

Columbus in the spring, maybe, but temperatures aside, Ohio State fans aren't the only things lending this area a central Ohio feel.

In Tempe, a block away from Sun Devil Stadium, site of the Fiesta Bowl, the Varsity Club is up and running. Yes, the Varsity Club, that staple of Lane Avenue and postgame hangout of many Buckeye fans. The rest of the year this locale is known as Bandersnatch Brew Pub. But this week it's the Varsity Club, complete with a sign outside and a marquee reading "Welcome Buckeye fans."

This is solace for many fans, who could be stewing with a bit of homesickness. It's even better for those Buckeye fans without tickets.

Left: Four-year-old Sean Gage, of Phoenix, sits on the shoulders of Ted Celeste, of Columbus, during a Buckeyes' pep rally in Tempe. *(Dante Smith/Newspaper Network of Central Ohio/Zanesville Times Recorder)*

Right: Judy Villard, of Mansfield, gets her face painted prior to a Buckeye pep rally the day before the Fiesta Bowl in Tempe, Ariz. Thousands of Ohio State fans turned out to support the team on the eve of their showdown with Miami. *(Dante Smith/Newspaper Network of Central Ohio/Zanesville Times Recorder)*

"We hope we can get tickets," said Linda Huffman, of Findlay. "But if we don't, there's always the Varsity Club."

Restaurateurs aren't the only local merchants enjoying the recent rush of Buckeye mania.

For the most part, stores are filled with Ohio State paraphernalia, while Miami stuff occupies the corners and crevices. Area store owners are turning into big Buckeye fans themselves, with anything OSU getting gobbled up by fans looking to remember this unbeaten season.

"It's been an exceptional day and a half so far," said Sid Rosenberg, part owner of Campus Corner on Mill Street in the heart of Tempe. "We knew Ohio State fans travel well and their great fans support their team. People have been buying a lot of Ohio State stuff, especially T-shirts. It's about 1,000-to-1 to Ohio State and Miami."

Rosenberg's assessment isn't the most scientific, but other Phoenix-area merchants did research some hard numbers before this week.

Melissa McCaig, owner of Sports Fan Marketing in Tempe, said she based her Fiesta Bowl week merchandise orders on information she received from travel agents. Those numbers said four Ohio State fans were booked to Arizona for every one Miami fan.

In accordance with this, her store had plenty of Buckeye gear.

"We've had a lot of Ohio State fans in here," McCaig said. "I would say our sales are up this year."

Below: Stephen Barthelmas, 12, of Columbus, tries to get a better vantage point during the Ohio State pep rally. *(Dante Smith/Newspaper Network of Central Ohio/Zanesville Times Recorder)*

So where are all the Miami fans? Theories abound.

"I think they're used to coming out and playing in the Fiesta Bowl," said Matt Gross, of Lancaster. " It's a lot bigger deal for us. Maybe they're spoiled."

How about another theory?

"There's probably more snowbirds from Ohio who live here anyway in the winter," said Lancaster's Jimmy Peck "People from Florida don't have to leave. They have the nice weather."

But back to the Buckeyes. Its hard to get away from them here, after all.

This is, from some reports, a better-than-normal showing for Buckeye fans, something Ashland's Lou Kauffman attributed in part to the fan's raging passion for Ohio State.

A shot at a national championship certainly doesn't hurt.

"I've been to every game since the Rose Bowl (in 1997) and this is the most I've ever seen," said Mandy Gross, of Lancaster. "It's amazing."

It's probably a good thing for Ohio State's players, too.

Kauffman thinks so. He's staying at the same hotel Ohio State's football team is, and said the team is greeted warmly by a group of fans every time it heads to an event or practice.

And a little moral support never hurt, especially for a team that's a big underdog.

"There's just a lot of red and gray to be seen," Kauffman said. "It's got to be good for these players to see all the supporters are there."

They're hard to miss. They are everywhere.

Left: Jimmy Peck, of Lancaster, shows off his Fiesta Bowl ticket. *(Jason J. Molyet/Newspaper Network of Central Ohio/Mansfield News Journal)*

Doss has chance to cap storybook career

By Jon Spencer
Newspaper Network of Central Ohio

COLUMBUS — If Ohio State safety Mike Doss had taken the money and run, as many expected when he called a news conference to announce his intentions last

Right: Strong safety Mike Doss celebrates a fourth-quarter fumble by Michigan in the Buckeyes' 14-9 win over the Wolverines.
(Jason J. Molyet/Newspaper Network of Central Ohio/Mansfield News Journal)

Jan. 9, he'd be finishing up his rookie season in the NFL. Instead, he is seeing his football career come full circle.

From winning a mythical national championship as a high school senior to playing for a national championship as a college senior.

From beginning his OSU career against the Miami Hurricanes in the 1999 Pigskin Classic to finishing his career against the 'Canes in the Jan. 3 Fiesta Bowl with the national title on the line.

"It's not ironic," said Doss, out of Canton McKinley High School. "This could be a storybook ending to my career."

Some would say his career is just beginning.

Staying at Ohio State for his final season enabled Doss to become only the seventh three-time All-American in school history. He was a finalist for the Thorpe Award, given to the nation's top defensive back, was named Big Ten Defensive Player of the Year by a vote of the coaches and earned Associated Press first-team All-America accolades.

"Mike Doss has made tremendous improvement," Ohio State coach Jim Tressel said. "At times, people questioned his (pass) coverage ability, but he was where he needed to be this season. His consistency was outstanding."

It would take a phenomenal effort against Miami for Doss to overtake All-America middle linebacker Matt Wilhelm and win the team tackle title for the third year in a row. But he does take a career-high 98 tackles into the bowl game and returned his only interception of the year 45 yards for a touchdown against Kent State.

"The ball didn't bounce his way as much," Tressel said, "so the big-play opportunities weren't there. But I think he improved significantly."

Defensive tackle Kenny Peterson, a boyhood friend of Doss, has seen a dramatic change in his teammate since they arrived at Ohio State together from Canton McKinley High School.

"It's been fun playing with him over the years," Peterson said. "Growing up, we played Pop Warner football together. The coach wanted to take Mike out, but he copped an attitude. 'Do you know who I am? I'm Mike Doss.' I thought, 'Oh, my God.' Everybody heard it. But he's matured a lot since then."

Self-confidence, however, has remained a key part of Doss' persona.

"He always wanted to be the big-play guy," Peterson said, "the guy who makes the difference. He's got that kind of personality. You get annoyed at times, but you've got no choice but to like him.

"He brings a lot of leadership; he's like a coach in the secondary. He's the big-play guy who electrifies the defense."

Doss had a huge decision to make after last season's Outback Bowl, which saw the Buckeyes lose 31-28 to South Carolina on a last-second field goal after rallying from a 28-0 deficit.

Leave for the NFL and he could afford to buy his mother, Diane Dixon, her dream house. Stay at Ohio State and he could help lead the Buckeyes to the national championship most observers felt was out of reach.

Peterson wasn't surprised that Doss opted for the latter during that tearful press conference.

"When he was deciding on whether to come back, we sat down and talked about it," Peterson said. "Mike told me, 'If I come back, I want to win a national championship.'

"At that point, you think anything is possible. That's the goal we set, and to accomplish that goal you've got to work hard."

It was fitting that Doss, a senior co-captain and, apparently, the biggest dreamer on the team, carried the Big Ten championship trophy into the postgame interview room after the Buckeyes clinched the title and a spot in the Fiesta Bowl with their 14-9 win over Michigan.

Doss left the room momentarily and returned sans jersey. Taped to the back of his shoulder pads was a faded newspaper article that ran the day after he decided to return to Ohio State. The headline read: "Doss does it for Mom."

"I wanted that on my back to remind me of why I came back," Doss said. "We had the No. 2 recruiting class in the country the year I came in.

"I came back to play with these guys I came in with, had blood, sweat and tears with. I couldn't pass that up. We always said that when it was our turn, we were going to do this. We always had faith we'd have a chance to play for the national championship."

Gamble an oddity in today's specialized game

By Jon Spencer
Newspaper Network of Central Ohio

COLUMBUS — He was dubbed Rip Van Gamble after revealing he slept 17 consecutive hours.

If there's one thing Ohio State sophomore Chris Gamble loves more than sleeping, it's playing football. In fact, it's that love for football that knocked him into dreamland from 8 p.m. to 1 the next afternoon after starting on both offense and defense for the first time in an Oct. 26 win over Penn State.

He deserved the beauty rest after making a touchdown-saving tackle in the opening minutes of the game and then returning a second-half interception 40 yards for OSU's only touchdown in the 13-7 victory.

If not for that

Right: Chris Gamble hauls in a catch during the second half of Ohio State's win against San Jose State.
(Trevor Jones/Gannett News Service/Coshocton Tribune)

performance and earlier game-saving end-zone interceptions against Cincinnati and Wisconsin, the Buckeyes would not be 13-0 and playing 12-0 Miami for the national championship in the Jan. 3 Fiesta Bowl.

"He's got God's gift, I guess," wide receiver Michael Jenkins said about Gamble becoming the first Buckeye to start both ways in over 40 years. "He enjoys doing it.

"That game against Penn State he was really tired and got cramps, but since then it doesn't seem to bother him."

Indeed, in the five games since this full-time starting flanker also became a starting cornerback to help out a troubled secondary, Gamble has been on the field for more than 100 plays three times, including a season-high 128 in the 23-16 overtime win at Illinois.

"It just speaks for the work ethic he has and the athlete he is," middle linebacker Matt Wilhelm said. "I honestly couldn't do it. I'm running from sideline to sideline. When we get a three-and-out, I'm sprinting off the field so I can sit down."

Since he also returns kickoffs and punts, Gamble rarely takes a seat. He is second on the team in receptions and first in interceptions (four).

"Obviously, Clarett is their headline guy," Minnesota

coach and OSU alum Glen Mason said of freshman tailback Maurice Clarett. "But to be able to compete at this level on offense, defense and in the kicking game, I don't know of a more complete football player in the country.

"If you're talking about making plays, big plays, and the ability to play a complete football game maybe like it was intended to be played, that's that young man."

Gamble's midseason transformation was stunning. He went from playing second fiddle to Jenkins in the receiving corps and playing a bit role on defense to becoming a first-team All-Big Ten cornerback and third-team All-American. Ohio State's players and coaches voted him co-MVP with quarterback Craig Krenzel.

"He's a special player," defensive coordinator Mark Dantonio said. "If you've got a wide side of the field corner who can cover, that allows everyone else on defense to play (less conservatively).

"He's got a lot of confidence and you've got to have a lot of confidence to play out there on an 'island' like he does. He has superior deep ball judgement, he's got toughness and he's got great quickness and anticipation."

Gamble has made an impression on at least one member of the 1942 Ohio State team that won the school's first national championship. Back then, it was common for players to start both ways.

"It's incredible today because you only train to go one way," said Bill Willis, an All-America tackle who went on to a Hall of Fame career with the Cleveland Browns. "Here's a guy who's not a big individual (6-2, 180), which means he has to be incredible to go both ways at such a high level.

"If the coach took you out and you didn't play 60 minutes

back when I played, you'd think something was wrong. Now you train mentally to just go on offense or defense. Yesteryear, you prided yourself on being just as good at both. You don't find many Gambles now."

Coach Jim Tressel noticed Gamble's coverage ability during a fun practice drill in which the wide receivers and defensive backs flip-flop roles. But he had no way of knowing if Gamble could handle going both ways or if it would rankle members of the secondary trying to crack the starting lineup.

"Anytime you make a personnel decision, there's a question of is it the right decision for the team and how will it affect your won-loss record," Tressel said. "How will someone else take that? Will someone take that as, 'You don't think I can do it.'" Those are all real risks."

As it turns out, the real risk would have been trying to move forward without Gamble on defense after starting cornerback Richard McNutt was lost with recurring ankle problems.

"Would we be 13-0 if we hadn't made the move? I don't know," Tressel said. "But Chris Gamble has made an impact. The players obviously felt he had a huge impact because they voted him co-MVP."

With six weeks to rest before meeting the defending national champions, Gamble says he's ready to play every down in the Fiesta Bowl. It's a dream challenge for him because he grew up 25 miles north of Miami in Sunrise, Fla.

"For me, it will be like playing a high school game on Friday night under the lights," Gamble said. "I'm going to give it my all and do what I usually do."

Besides, he'll have eight months to sleep before Ohio State's next game.

Commentary:
Why the belief that Miami is invincible?

By Larry Phillips
Newspaper Network of Central Ohio

The Miami Hurricanes must be a far different team than the unit I've seen this season.

I've watched Larry Coker's club four times, and agree they are a very good college football team. They deserve to be ranked No. 1.

Larry Phillips

But I've also seen enough to know Miami is not without flaws. This is a team that was tested by Florida State, West Virginia, Pittsburgh, and even hapless Rutgers. That's what makes it hard to fathom why so many think Ohio State can't challenge the mighty Hurricanes when the two tangle in the Fiesta Bowl.

Where I see a squad that is nowhere near as good as last year's national champions, which had five first-round NFL draft picks, others see a perfect, unbeatable machine.

"There is not an NFL team with more team speed than the Hurricanes," New York Giants general manager Ernie Accorsi said recently.

If this were a track meet, Ohio State would be outclassed. This isn't a track meet.

That hardly seems to matter to ESPN blowhard Trev Alberts. On a recent ESPN.com chat, Alberts, who has poor-mouthed Ohio State and deemed the Buckeyes second to Iowa in the Big Ten all season, said he would give Jim Tressel's squad no credit should they to pull off a miraculous upset and somehow slip past Miami.

Steve (Orlando): "Trev, if Ohio State beats Miami, will you still insist that they're not the best team in the country?"

Trev Alberts: "Yeah. Because they are not going to beat Miami. If Miami loses, it will be because Miami beat itself. I don't see that happening. Until you beat the best team in your conference, don't tell me you can beat Miami. You have four weeks to come up with a passing game!

"OSU has a very good defense, a very good running game. The passing game is where you falter. That is why you are not in the upper tier that I just talked about."

Gee, Ohio State isn't in the upper tier of college football? Then Tressel must have done the greatest coaching job in history. Somehow OSU went unbeaten in a conference that has four teams ranked in the top 12. The Buckeyes also reached the national championship game with this sorry bunch.

Unfortunately, that kind of idiocy isn't uncommon.

In the Sporting News, Tim Brando called Ohio State a bad 12-0 team and said, "When they lose to Michigan they'll be a bad 12-1 team."

Instead, OSU bounced the ninth-ranked Wolverines 14-9. Yet Brando still was unimpressed. He picked Miami to hammer the Buckeyes 48-10 in the Fiesta Bowl.

Too bad Brando is a stranger. I'd love to lighten his wallet. A line of "friends" probably has already formed to gladly take his 38 points, and soon after his money.

The fact is Ohio State hasn't allowed 48 points in a game since 1994. The Buckeyes have allowed only 41 points combined in their past five games, while playing in a much better conference than the Big East, which has one other team besides Miami in the top 20 (15th-ranked West Virginia).

At least one Hurricane has bought the bull — and perhaps the horns.

Tight end Kellen Winslow Jr. told the New York Daily News: "Nobody has our talent.

"We're way too fast for Ohio State. What conference are they in? The Big Ten? Ohio State and Nebraska are both power teams. It'll be like Nebraska was last year (a 37-14 Miami victory at the Rose Bowl). Nobody can hang with our speed."

Do you think that comment will get the attention of All-American safety Mike Doss and All-American linebacker Matt Wilhelm?

Make no mistake, Miami wields an exciting, explosive offense and perhaps the best running back in the country in Willis McGahee. They have a very good quarterback in Ken Dorsey and a strong receiver in Andre Johnson.

But Miami also has the 70th-ranked defense in the nation. Pittsburgh, Florida State and West Virginia each ran all over the Hurricanes. Not incidentally, all of those teams had a chance to beat Miami. In fact, the four-loss Seminoles should have done it. They missed a short field goal at the gun that would have won the game.

With Maurice Clarett returning to health, Miami is about to see the best running back it has faced all year. Ohio State has a better defense than anything the Hurricanes have seen as well. OSU has another edge in kicking, with punter Andy Groom and placekicker Mike Nugent.

I'm not saying the Buckeyes are the better team. I'm not saying they will win this game. They are a double-digit underdog for a reason.

But if defenses truly win championships, and if special teams are as important as coaches and analysts constantly tell us, then why is Ohio State deemed such a bad team by so many people?

Game day is here: Will Clarett be distracted or motivated?

By Jon Spencer
Newspaper Network of Central Ohio

PHOENIX — Ohio State tailback Maurice Clarett has been off-limits to reporters the last two days, leaving everyone to wonder whether he will channel some

Right: OSU running back Maurice Clarett breaks free for a touchdown against Texas Tech.
(Jason J. Molyet/Newspaper Network of Central Ohio/Mansfield News Journal)

of the anger he has directed at his school into a great performance against run-challenged Miami in the Fiesta Bowl.

Clarett says he's 100 percent physically after dealing with a shoulder stinger the last half of the regular season. But is he 100 percent mentally after blaming the school for not finding a way to cut through bureaucratic tape and get him home for a friend's funeral?

"One never knows where someone is in the grieving process," coach Jim Tressel said. "He's going through it. This might be a fortunate moment in that he has a lot of family and friends and coaches around, and I think he's working hard to handle that situation."

The "D" word has been thrown around a lot in recent days. But instead of talking about the dynasty Miami has forged during a 34-game winning streak, everyone seems focused on the potential distraction Clarett has caused his team with his emotional outbursts.

His rants have ranged from complaining that "football is more important than life" at Ohio State to calling school officials "liars" in the way they handled his situation.

"I'm very confident in the way our guys feel about playing this game," Tressel said. "I don't think when you have a group of 105 players and 20-some coaches and managers you ever pretend everyone's on the same page. But I feel good about how they feel about one another ... I feel good about our preparation and now you have to see if that turns into getting it done (in the game)."

The Buckeyes likely will need Clarett, who has rushed for a school freshman record 1,190 yards, at the top of his game to win Ohio State's first consensus national championship since 1968. OSU needs Clarett and the clock to keep moving against a Miami defense that has been vulnerable to the run. The Bucks need to limit the Hurricanes' quick-strike opportunities.

The 'Canes, favored by two touchdowns, have averaged 1:58 for their 67 touchdown drives this season. Thirty-seven touchdowns were scored in less than two minutes and 18 took less than a minute.

"Sometimes they only have the ball a couple of plays and they score," OSU cornerback Dustin Fox said. "Our goal is to get more third downs. It seems like they either score real fast or it's three-and-out.

"We've got to take that challenge and not allow the big play. It will be fun to get on the field with them and see how we stack up."

Ohio State doesn't make its 40-yard dash times known, but Fox, tailback Maurice Hall and wide receiver/cornerback Chris Gamble are said to be the team's quickest players.

At Miami, tailback Willis McGahee (a Heisman Trophy finalist) runs a 4.26, receiver Andre Johnson (co-MVP in last year's national championship game) runs a 4.34 and team-best 10.5 in the 100 meters, and receiver Roscoe

Parrish runs a 4.35. Andrew Williams, a 6-4, 262-pound defensive end, was the anchor on Hinds Community College's 4-by-100 relay team and 6-4, 271-pound end Jerome McDougle ran the second leg on that team.

"Our entire track team are football players," Miami coach Larry Coker said. "A week or two after last year's Rose Bowl (a 37-14 Miami win over Nebraska for the national crown), McGahee and Johnson ran at a Big East track meet. Andre got first in the 55 meters and Willis came in third. Without even working out ... against real track people."

Miami thrives on the big play. Ohio State denies the big play. The Buckeyes have allowed only 11 runs of more than 15 yards this season and four of those were in the first half against Wisconsin. They lead the nation in giving up only four rushing touchdowns and have allowed only two touchdowns (one rushing, one passing) in their last five games.

Remarkably, the opposition has scored touchdowns on only nine of 36 trips inside the 20-yard line.

"Is it structural or attitude? I'd like to think it's a little bit of both," defensive coordinator Mark Dantonio said. "I'd like to think it shows the character of the players and the way they've handled themselves down there (in the red zone).

"Three things I ask our players to do consistently — we've got to play with toughness, with great effort, and we've got to know what to do. It's a matter of getting our mind right."

But is Maurice Clarett's mind right?

Only one thing left to say: Champions

By Jon Spencer
Newspaper Network of Central Ohio

TEMPE, Ariz. – Ohio State fans already had waited 34 years for an undisputed national championship. Certainly Buckeye Nation could hold its collective breath for a couple of nerve-wracking overtime periods in the Fiesta Bowl.

Coming back from the brink with two fourth-down conversions in the first OT, the Buckeyes rode Maurice Clarett's five-yard run and an ensuing goal-line stand to a 31-24 double-overtime victory over the Miami Hurricanes in Sun Devil Stadium.

The improbable ending to an improbable OSU season delivered the underrated Buckeyes to their first consensus title since 1968 and dethroned the defending champs, snapping the Hurricanes' 34-game winning streak.

Left: Ohio State coaches and players storm the field after the final play of the Fiesta Bowl win over Miami.
(Jason J. Molyet/Newspaper Network of Central Ohio/Mansfield News Journal)

Right: Ohio State defensive back Donnie Nickey holds up the top of the Fiesta Bowl trophy as Mike Doss and Matt Wilhelm watch. *(Dante Smith/Newspaper Network of Central Ohio/Zanesville Times Recorder)*

Ohio State became the first major college team to complete a 14-0 season and handed coach Jim Tressel his fifth national championship in only his second year at the school. His first four titles came at Division

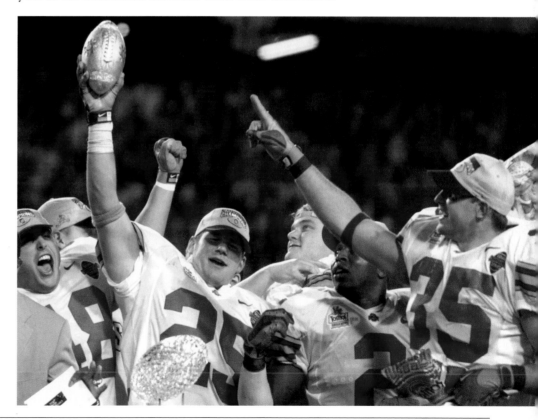

Right: Buckeye defensive lineman Tim Anderson hits Miami quarterback Ken Dorsey.
(Jason J. Molyet/Newspaper Network of Central Ohio/Mansfield News Journal)

I-AA Youngstown State.

"We've got the best damn band in the land," shouted Tressel, his voice hoarse during the trophy presentation at midfield. "Now we've got the best damn team in the land."

Miami (12-1), a two-touchdown favorite, had the ball first in the first OT and scored when tight end Kellen Winslow Jr. went over the top of nickel back Will Allen for a seven-yard touchdown catch.

Ohio State made it 24-all on a one-yard keeper by quarterback Craig Krenzel after the Buckeyes had survived two fourth-down plays. Michael Jenkins made a 17-yard catch on fourth and 14 from the 29 and then Miami cornerback Glenn Sharpe was called for interfering with Chris Gamble on fourth and three from the five.

After Maurice Clarett gave Ohio State the lead in the second overtime, the 'Canes moved to a first-and-goal at the two and had two cracks at the end zone from the one. With star tailback Willis McGahee out with a knee injury, fullback Quadtrine Hill got stuffed on third down. On fourth down, linebacker Cie Grant broke free on the blitz and forced an off-balance throw by quarterback Ken Dorsey that safety Donnie Nickey knocked to the ground.

"That's the way it's been all year," said Krenzel, named the offensive

Above: Mike Doss brings down Miami running back Willis McGahee. *(Jason J. Molyet/ Newspaper Network of Central Ohio/Mansfield News Journal)*

Left: Dustin Fox levels Miami tight end Kellen Winslow Jr. *(Jason J. Molyet/Newspaper Network of Central Ohio/Mansfield News Journal)*

MVP for leading OSU through all sorts of mine fields despite completing only seven of 21 passes and throwing two interceptions. "We make plays in close games when we have to."

It looked like the Buckeyes would

Above: OSU's Mike Doss runs back a Ken Dorsey interception in the second quarter. *(Jason J. Molyet/Newspaper Network of Central Ohio/Mansfield News Journal)*

Right: Mike Doss celebrates after running back an interception deep into Miami territory that set up OSU's first touchdown. *(Jason J. Molyet/Newspaper Network of Central Ohio/Mansfield News Journal)*

win the game in regulation when Miami wideout Roscoe Parrish fumbled at the OSU 18 with five minutes remaining. But Parrish atoned for that error with a 49-yard punt return that set up a game-tying, 40-yard field goal by Todd Sievers as time expired.

Miami took an early 7-0 lead on Parrish's 25-yard reception, but Dorsey's second-quarter implosion in the face of relentless pressure led to two OSU touchdowns and paved the way to only his second loss in 40 games as a starter.

The Buckeyes rattled Dorsey into two interceptions and a fumble in the pivotal second period. All three turnovers were committed in Miami territory, leading to OSU's 14-7 halftime edge.

A wild sequence of giveaway-takeaway on OSU's first series of the third period saw the Buckeyes pad their lead on a 44-yard field goal by Mike Nugent. A 57-yard pass from Krenzel to Gamble carried OSU to the six, but on the next play Krenzel's pass in the end zone for tight end Ben Hartsock was picked off by safety Sean Taylor.

Taylor took it back 28 yards,

only to have the ball wrestled from his hands by Clarett before they both tumbled to the ground. The Buckeyes had new life and, soon after, a 17-7 lead.

The 'Canes cut the deficit to 17-14 on a nine-yard TD run by McGahee (67 yards, 20 carries), but he would retire early when a knee injury sent him to the

sidelines with 11:39 left in regulation.

Still, Miami overcame the loss of the Heisman Trophy finalist to force the first overtime in championship game history.

Ohio State got off to a rough start, getting flagged for illegal substitution on the game's first play from scrimmage and failing

Above: Maurice Clarett pushes into the end zone for his first touchdown of the game, in the second quarter. *(Jason J. Molyet/Newspaper Network of Central Ohio/Mansfield News Journal)*

Right: Michael Jenkins, left, and Rob Sims, right, help Maurice Clarett celebrate his first touchdown of the game. *(Jason J. Molyet/Newspaper Network of Central Ohio/Mansfield News Journal)*

to muster a first down.

But the defense meant business from the get-go, sacking Dorsey twice on the first series after the two-time Heisman Trophy finalist had been sacked only 11 times all season.

Dorsey rebounded from that jittery start to complete eight of 10 passes for 119 yards in the first period, including the 25-yard scoring toss to Parrish on third and 12.

An assist went to McGahee on the play for shoving

aside Nickey as he came on the blitz up the middle.

Undeterred, OSU's defense kept hounding Dorsey, forcing two interceptions and a fumble in the second quarter.

A pick by Fox in Miami territory went for naught when the Buckeyes faked a field goal on fourth and one from the 17. Holder Andy Groom ran with the snap but was stopped just short of the first down marker.

The Ohio State defense set up the offense again when strong safety Mike

Doss intercepted a deflection off the hands of Miami's Andre Johnson and returned it 35 yards to the UM 17. Krenzel was stopped on third and goal from the one, but he spun in on fourth down as the Buckeyes knotted the score at 7.

On the first play after the ensuing kickoff, Dorsey fumbled on a sack by Kenny Peterson and Darrion Scott recovered at 14. Held to zero yards on seven carries to that point, Clarett went seven yards for the go-ahead score at halftime.

Right: Glenn Sharpe is called for pass interference on Chris Gamble in the first overtime. The controversial call kept OSU alive. *(Jason J. Molyet/Newspaper Network of Central Ohio/Mansfield News Journal)*

Below: Craig Krenzel, Maurice Clarett, Jim Tressel and Ben Hartsock huddle up during the second overtime. *(Dante Smith/Newspaper Network of Central Ohio/Zanesville Times Recorder)*

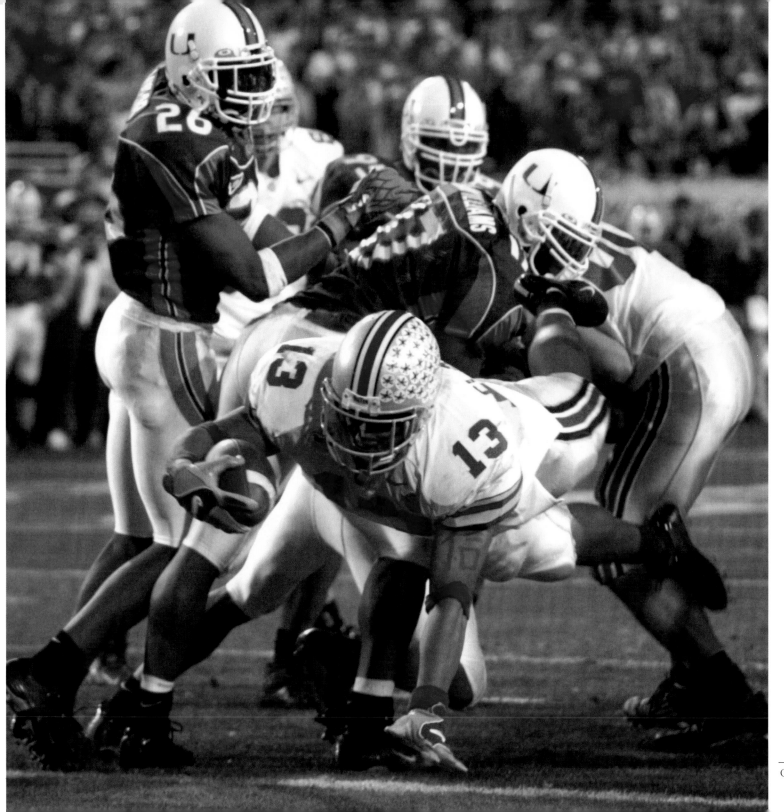

Left: Maurice Clarett scores the winning touchdown in double overtime.
(Dante Smith/Newspaper Network of Central Ohio/ Zanesville Times Recorder)

Left: Ohio State defensive lineman Kenny Peterson is lost in a sea of confetti during the celebration.
(Jason J. Molyet/Newspaper Network of Central Ohio/Mansfield News Journal)

Below: Players, coaches and fans sing "Carmen Ohio" to celebrate the Buckeye victory.
(Jason J. Molyet/Newspaper Network of Central Ohio/Mansfield News Journal)

Above: Former Ohio State standout Archie Griffin holds a copy of the Mansfield News Journal declaring the Buckeye victory. *(Jason J. Molyet/ Newspaper Network of Central Ohio/Mansfield News Journal)*

Left: Offensive lineman T.J. Downing and receiver Santonio Holmes celebrate the win. *(Jason J. Molyet/Newspaper Network of Central Ohio/Mansfield News Journal)*

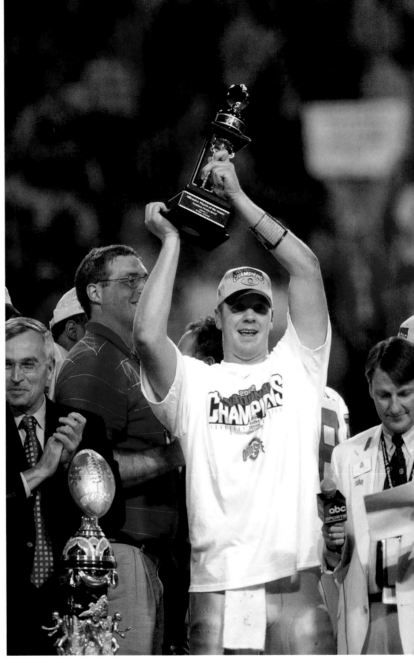

Above: OSU quarterback Craig Krenzel holds up the offensive MVP trophy from the Fiesta Bowl. *(Jason J. Molyet/Newspaper Network of Central Ohio/Mansfield News Journal)*

Left: OSU head coach Jim Tressel gets to the point — OSU is No. 1. *(Jason J. Molyet/Newspaper Network of Central Ohio/Mansfield News Journal)*

Commentary:
Reflecting on the insanity of a classic game

By Jon Spencer
Newspaper Network of Central Ohio

PHOENIX — Climbing more than a mile of jagged rock up Squaw Peak here in the Valley of the Sun was harrowing for a city boy from Ohio without his water bottle. But it was nowhere near as arduous as the mountain Jim Tressel's Ohio State Buckeyes ascended to a national championship.

That doesn't mean I can't relate to the suffocating pressure they felt in the Fiesta Bowl.

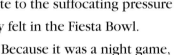

Jon Spencer

Because it was a night game, I was working under extremely tight deadlines. The vise tightened as the game went into one overtime and then another, becoming a full-blown marathon classic.

The gameplan set for me was to send the first version of my game story back to Ohio as soon as the scoreboard clock struck 0:00. That meant I spent the entire second half of maybe the greatest college football game ever furiously pecking away at my keyboard and peering over the top of my laptop at yet another in a series of remarkable plays.

In situations such as this, I determine the greatness of what I'm witnessing by how many times I have to rework what I've written. By that barometer — by any barometer — this game was off-the-charts incredible.

A game-tying, 40-yard field goal by the Miami Hurricanes as time expired in regulation, by a kicker who had converted only four of 11 previous kicks from that far, after OSU had tried to freeze him with back-to-back timeouts?

Two improbable fourth-down conversions by the Buckeyes in the first OT, with their season down to a last gasp each time and apparently over at one point until a penalty flag belatedly came fluttering to earth from the back of the end zone?

A magnificent goal-line stand by Ohio State in the second OT as one of the most prolific offenses in college football history failed to score on four cracks from inside the two?

Are you kidding me?

The lead of my story, like the tide of this game, changed so often I lost count.

Originally, I thought I'd write about Maurice Clarett and how he'd remind us with the nation watching that he is just as adept at running with the football as he is at running his mouth. But despite scoring two TDs, including the game-winner, and stripping the ball from a defender on a pivotal double turnover, Miami's freakishly fast defense limited Clarett to 47 yards on 23 carries.

Scratch that idea.

Then I was going to lead with how the game was put in the hands of Miami quarterback Ken Dorsey, and how that gameplan by OSU worked to perfection. In the second quarter, the Buckeyes intercepted him twice and knocked the ball from his grasp another time, converting two of those three turnovers into a 14-7 halftime lead that grew to 17-7.

But then Dorsey started finding slick tight end Kellen Winslow Jr. with regularity and the 'Canes were right back in the game.

Scratch that idea.

Then I was going to lead with how Miami wide receiver Roscoe Parrish went from hero to goat to hero in this topsy-turvy encounter. He staked the 'Canes to an early lead with his 25-yard TD reception, put a stake through their heart by fumbling at the OSU 18 with five minutes showing and Miami down by three, and revived his team with a 50-yard punt return to set up the tying field goal.

But when Miami blew its lead in the first OT, Parrish became nothing more than a footnote in history.

Scratch that idea.

At that point, I gave up and decided that, deadlines or no deadlines, I was powerless to do anything but sit back and watch like Joe Fan at home in his recliner. With one difference. From my perspective literally atop Sun Devil Stadium — I was outside on the roof — the game was as breathtaking as the sun-setting skyline view of the mountains framing the battlefield.

And when I say battlefield, I'm not using the word flippantly.

A Miami program that earned notoriety in its last Fiesta Bowl appearance for donning battle fatigues should have left on the bus in battle fatigues.

Judging from the tears, the Hurricanes knew they had been in a war. A trail of tears followed superb tailback Willis McGahee off on a cart after his left knee blew up on a hard-to-watch fourth-quarter collision with OSU's Will Allen.

Dorsey wailed like a baby in the locker room after losing for only the second time in 40 games as a starter and for the first time in 35 games.

His roommate, All-America center Brett Romberg, hadn't allowed a sack in his entire four-year career. The game was barely 10 minutes old when he allowed his first.

The Buckeyes sacked Dorsey four times. They forced five turnovers, causing three fumbles on blind-side hits. They beat the high-and-mighty 'Canes 31-24 despite completing only seven passes and mustering only 14 first downs.

"I don't know if they'll get 'it' until more time passes," Tressel said of his players' monumental achievement. "I can picture some of them going, 'We're the national champions. We're the national champions. We did it. We did it.' It will be something very, very special.

"But I hope what they get from it is what it takes to be a champion — all the people that are important, all the things that have to be done, all the lessons learned. If they get that, I don't care if they ever get what it means to be a national champion. I hope they get the lessons."

I got my lesson. When writing on deadline, never try to think one step ahead of these cardiac Buckeyes.

Commentary:
I should have known better than to doubt the Buckeyes

By Jason Maddux
Newspaper Network of Central Ohio

OK, I'll admit it.

I doubted the Buckeyes.

Not in a Trev Alberts, all-season-long kind of way.

But I didn't think they had much of a chance to win the Fiesta Bowl.

I'm not a Buckeye fatalist or anything. Once the season got rolling, I realized they were going to win a lot of games. I even thought they would beat Michigan by a couple of touchdowns.

Jason Maddux

That's not their style, though. Causing their fans to forget to breathe is their style.

Now it's the style of a national champion.

I sat in the press box watching them beat Cincinnati and Penn State and Michigan. I saw them beat Purdue and Illinois. I knew magic was floating around this team.

But still, I doubted their Fiesta Bowl chances.

Speed kills, I told one person. Remember the 1998 Sugar Bowl vs. Florida State? That was a brutal display of speed that doomed OSU.

This would be a similar game, or so I thought. I bought in to the national media hype that the 'Canes were just too fast. I said the score would be somewhere around 38-17 Miami ... if the Buckeyes could even get 17.

That wasn't the case. Actually, the Buckeyes did score 17 in regulation, though, so I was partly right.

Speaking of predictions, many people in the Ohio media picked the Buckeyes to win. My good friend and colleague Jon Spencer, who covers the Buckeyes for the Newspaper Network of Central Ohio, predicted a 24-20 OSU victory.

Homerism, I thought. You're getting caught up in the hoopla and fan frenzy and picking with your heart. I should have known better that to think that of Spence. He's covered the Buckeyes since Earle Bruce's last season, and he's not a "pick-with-your-heart" type of guy.

The Buckeyes won by doing things against Miami in the Fiesta Bowl that I did not think they could do. I didn't think any team could stop the Miami running game like the Buckeyes did. Or hit quarterback Ken Dorsey as often as they did. Or force five turnovers like they did.

They were outgained. They were left for dead in overtime. They still won.

They won seven games this season by seven points or less. That is truly amazing. They didn't have the best individual talent. They had the best team.

Jim Tressel should quit right now. How can he possibly follow this up? He has proven that being a winner translates to any level. ESPN GameDay's Chris Fowler jokes about "Sen. Tressel" keeping his "constituency happy." They're happy right now. I think Mike DeWine and George Voinovich can sleep easy at night. Tressel might go to Washington, but it only would be to accept congratulations from the president.

Back to Alberts for just a minute. He beat up on the Buckeyes pretty good all year, saying Iowa was the best team in the Big Ten and that even if Ohio State somehow won the Fiesta Bowl, it would be because Miami beat itself. "I don't see that happening. Until you beat the best team in your conference, don't tell me you can beat Miami," he said during an ESPN chat session in December.

On ESPN.com after the game, he still wasn't exactly praising the Buckeyes, saying that you "have to take your hat off to college football after this game."

What about taking your hat off to the Buckeyes? He did call the game an instant classic, and that Tressel and his staff deserve congratulations. He even said that he expects OSU to start next season ranked No. 1 with the players they have coming back.

Gee, thanks Trev. You just can't admit you blew it, can you?

So what is next? We'll bask in this one for quite awhile. We should.

And you know us Buckeye fans. We're reasonable. We'll only expect four or five championships a decade now that the monkey is off our backs.

Just 238 days until Washington visits the 'Shoe for the 2003 season opener ...

Fiesta Bowl by the Numbers

Box Score

#2 Ohio State vs #1 Miami (Jan. 3, 2003 at Tempe, Ariz.)

Score by Quarters	1	2	3	4	OT	Score	
Ohio State	0	14	3	0	14	31	Record: (14-0)
Miami	7	0	7	3	7	24	Record: (12-1)

Scoring Summary:

1st 04:09 MIAMI - Parrish, Roscoe 25 yd pass from Dorsey, Ken (Sievers, Todd kick), 5 plays, 52 yards, 2:12 time of posession, OSU 0 - MIAMI 7

2nd 02:28 OSU - Krenzel, Craig 1 yd run (Nugent, Mike kick), 7-17 3:08, OSU 7 - MIAMI 7
01:10 OSU - Clarett, Maurice 7 yd run (Nugent, Mike kick), 2-14 1:05, OSU 14 - MIAMI 7

3rd 08:33 OSU - Nugent, Mike 44 yd field goal, 4-1 2:00, OSU 17 - MIAMI 7
02:11 MIAMI - McGahee, Willis 9 yd run (Sievers, Todd kick), 7-55 2:54, OSU 17 - MIAMI 14

4th 00:00 MIAMI - Sievers, Todd 40 yd field goal, 4-3, 2:02, OSU 17 - MIAMI 17

OT MIAMI - Winslow, Kellen 7 yd pass from Dorsey, Ken (Sievers, Todd kick), 5-25, OSU 17 - MIAMI 24
OSU - Krenzel, Craig 1 yd run (Nugent, Mike kick), 10-25, OSU 24 - MIAMI 24

2nd OT OSU - Clarett, Maurice 5 yd run (Nugent, Mike kick), 5-25, OSU 31 - MIAMI 24

Statistics

	OSU	MIAMI
FIRST DOWNS	14	19
RUSHES-YARDS (NET)	52-145	33-65
PASSING YDS (NET)	122	304
Passes Att-Comp-Int	21-7-2	44-29-2
TOTAL OFFENSE PLAYS-YARDS	73-267	77-369
Punt Returns-Yards	1-1	2-56
Kickoff Returns-Yards	1-15	1-39
Interception Returns-Yards	2-47	2-28
Punts (Number-Avg)	6-47.7	4-43.2
Fumbles-Lost	0-0	3-3
Penalties-Yards	9-49	6-30
Possession Time	31:27	28:33
Third-Down Conversions	6 of 18	6 of 18
Fourth-Down Conversions	2 of 3	1 of 2
Red-Zone Scores-Chances	2-4	2-2
Sacks By: Number-Yards	4-18	1-4

RUSHING: Ohio State-Krenzel, Craig 19-81; Clarett, Maurice 23-47; Ross, Lydell 9-17; Groom, Andy 1-0. Miami-McGahee, Willis 20-67; Payton, Jarrett 8-17; Hill, Quadtrine 1-0; Dorsey, Ken 4-minus 19.

PASSING: Ohio State-Krenzel, Craig 7-21-2-122. Miami-Dorsey, Ken 28-43-2-296; Crudup, Derrick 1-1-0-8.

RECEIVING: Ohio State-Jenkins, Michael 4-45; Gamble, Chris 2-69; Vance, Chris 1-8. Miami-Winslow, Kellen 11-122; Parrish, Roscoe 5-70; Johnson, Andre 4-54; Sands, Ethenic 3-34; McGahee, Willis 3-5; Hill, Quadtrine 1-8; Payton, Jarrett 1-7; Geathers, Jason 1-4.

INTERCEPTIONS: Ohio State-Fox, Dustin 1-12; Doss, Mike 1-35. Miami-Taylor, Sean 2-28.

FUMBLES (Lost): Ohio State-None. Miami-Dorsey, Ken 1-1; Taylor, Sean 1-1; Parrish, Roscoe 1-1.

SACKS (Unassisted-Assisted): Ohio State-Peterson, Kenny 2-0; Smith, Will 1-0; Fraser, Simon 1-0. Miami-Green, Jamaal 1-0.

TACKLES (Unassisted-Assisted): Ohio State-Wilhelm, Matt 6-4; Doss, Mike 3-6; Smith, Will 6-2; Fox, Dustin 5-2; Grant, Cie 4-3; Peterson, Kenny 4-1; Nickey, Donnie 3-2; Allen, Will 3-2; Gamble, Chris 3-2; Reynolds, Robert 3-1; Anderson, Tim 1-3; Thompson, David 0-3; Scott, Darrion 1-0; Everett, Tyler 1-0; Moore, Steven 1-0; Fraser, Simon 1-0; Clarett, Maurice 1-0; Groom, Andy 0-1; TEAM 0-1; Kudla, Mike 0-1. Miami-Vilma, Jonathan 5-9; Sikes, Maurice 2-10; Taylor, Sean 2-9; Williams, D.J. 3-5; McIntosh, Roger 2-6; Walters, Matt 4-3; Rolle, Antrel 2-2; Harris, Orien 1-3; Green, Jamaal 2-1; Joseph, William 2-1; Haji-Rasouli, S 2-0; Williams, And. 1-1; Sharpe, Glenn 1-1; McDougle, J. 1-1; Scott, James 1-0; Marshall, Al 1-0; McGahee, Willis 1-0; Wilfork, Vince 1-0.

Stadium: Sun Devil Stadium   **Attendance:** 77,502
Kickoff time: 6:21   **End of Game:** 10:17   **Total elapsed time:** 3:56
Officials: Referee: Randy Christal **Umpire:** Steve Storie
Linesman: Don Kapral **Line judge:** Derick Bowers **Back judge:** John Robinson
Field judge: Terry Porter **Side judge:** Brad Van Vark **Scorer:** John Olson
Temperature: 70   **Wind:** W9   **Weather:** Beautiful

How we saw it:
Front page coverage of the Buckeye victory

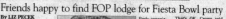

BUCKEYE CHAMPIONSHIP EXTRA!

The Advocate

Saturday, January 4, 2003

35 cents

Ohio State wins 2-OT thriller to become undisputed

CHAMPS!

CLASSIC CHAMPIONSHIP
- Buckeyes convert two title-saving fourth downs before stopping Hurricanes' final-play prayer.
- Quarterback Craig Krenzel outruns everyone on way to two OT touchdown drives.
- Clarett's steal saves three Buckeye points.

See game coverage on Page 2A

DEFENSE WINS TITLES
- Buckeyes shut down Miami's big guns, force five turnovers.
- Hurricanes' Dorsey struggles.
- Fiesta Bowl grade card for OSU.
- Ohio State notebook.

See in-depth analysis on Page 3A

CELEBRATION!
- Fourth-straight Buckeye thriller leaves local fans hysterical.
- Everyday life halts for title game throughout Licking County.
- Plans for Columbus celebration, team's return not finalized.

See local coverage on Page 4A

Weekend

USA WEEKEND — 2003 A Super Year

Today in USA WEEKEND

Happy birthday Ohio — Coming Monday

New bad boy needed — Opinion, Page 4A

Sports, Page 2B — Showdown

Telegraph-Forum

www.bucyrustelegraphforum.com

SATURDAY-SUNDAY, JANUARY 4-5, 2003 • SERVING BUCYRUS AND CRAWFORD COUNTY • 50 CENTS

Forecast

Mostly cloudy, chance of snow. See 2A.

Good day

In the hallway outside the Ohio State locker room, Archie Griffin, the Buckeyes' two-time Heisman Trophy winner, grabbed coach Jim Tressel in a long hug.

Rex Kern, the quarterback for the Buckeyes the last time they won a national championship 34 years ago, quietly watched the celebration and compared it to that one so long ago.

"This was just as good," he said. "Our kids don't know when to quit. They never quit. They played with class."

On Monday

The last word

The T-F puts the Buck's amazing season to bed with six special pages of coverage.

Happy 200, Ohio

Ohio observes its bicentennial this year and the T-F will honor the event with a special feature each Monday focusing on interesting facts about Ohio, its history, people and places.

On the Web

National and world stories are updated every 15 minutes on our Web site, www.bucyrustelegraphforum.com.

Deaths

Kimberly S. Butler
Barbara A. Rader
Paul W. Starlin
Obituaries, Page 2A

Lottery

MegaMillions
6-14-28-37-46
Mega Ball 3
Buckeye 5
4-19-21-29-33
Pick 3: 600 Day: 389
Pick 4: 7535 Day: 4422

Index

Lights & Sirens   2A
Local News   3A
Opinion   4A
Community   5A
Faith   7A
TV Listings   8-9A
Dear Abby   8A
Sports   1-4B
Classified   4B
Comics   9B

A Gannett newspaper

Fans cheer Buckeye victory

OSU spirit seen all over city

Telegraph-Forum staff

All over the city, people showed their OSU spirit Friday, willing the Bucks to victory over the top-ranked Hurricanes to claim their first national title since the 1969 Rose Bowl.

"Go Mate Deer," read First Federal Bank's traffic-stopping marquis all day long.

By 8 p.m., the faithful were parked in front of TVs, tuning into radios or checking workstation computers to follow the game.

And what a game it was.

At the American Legion at 123 E. Rensselaer St., members clad in scarlet and gray snacked on chicken wings and Tostitos, clanged

See FANS/Page 3A

T-F photos by Beth Thompson

Left, the crowd gathered at the home of Bill Barker, 1550 Rosedale Ave., cheers as the Ohio State Buckeyes win the national championship at the Fiesta Bowl on Friday night. Above, dressed in his OSU jersey, Clayton Schifer, 2, hugs his football as he watches the Buckeyes take home the big trophy.

Crestline couple have first '03 baby

By Charma Messer
Telegraph-Forum staff

Crawford County's New Year baby took its sweet time, although when she arrived, she was early.

Confused?

Abigail Brooke Potter wasn't due for four more days, so when her appearance at 7:33 p.m. Thursday at Galion Community Hospital brought her the unexpected Baby New Year title, parents James and Tabitha Potter were surprised.

Abigail issued forth after 11 hours of labor, checking in at 6 pounds and 20.5 inches.

With Dr. Tyler Huggins out of town — cheering the Buckeyes at the Fiesta Bowl — the baby was delivered by nurse midwife Kris Jones.

Great-grandma Lola Powell of Galion said that although Abigail wasn't for the family, she was the first one to have a title at birth.

Abigail is the first child for the Potters, who reside in Crestline.

T-F photo by Beth Thompson

Crawford County's first baby of 2003, Abigail Brooke Potter, rests in her mother's arms. Tabitha Potter gave birth to Abigail on Thursday at Galion Community Hospital.

cmesser@nncogannett.com
419-563-9226

Bush rallies nervous troops

FORT HOOD, Texas (AP) — Fired-up soldiers cheered President Bush Friday as he told them they may be called into combat "to secure our country and to keep the peace."

Privately, they showed more anxiety about the prospect of being sent to fight Iraq.

If it comes to war, "this generation of Americans is ready," Bush said. "We accept the burden of leadership. We act in the cause of peace and freedom. And in that cause we will prevail."

Fort Hood is home to some 42,000 troops — the most at any American military base. More than 25,000 fought in the 1991 Gulf War, and soldiers here would almost certainly be deployed in another war with Iraq.

While the soldiers Bush met here Friday brimmed with confidence, others confessed in interviews they are nervous.

"Anybody who said he is not nervous or scared is lying to himself," said Spc.

Eric Wilkerson, who has an 18-month-old daughter and a fiancee.

"I've always wanted to go to war, but now that it's here, just the thought of getting killed make me not want to go," said Spc. Cody Newby.

Sgt. Santos Martinez said his mother had served in Vietnam, and her experience had acquainted him with the perils of war. But, he said: "I signed up. I volunteered to serve. If my country says it's worth it, then personal thoughts aside, I say it's worth it."

Others, speaking privately, expressed doubts about the need for war with Iraq.

Bush delivered his nationwide while emphasizing war is a last resort. As he laid out his case, the boisterous crowd of 4,000 camouflage-clad soldiers fell silent.

Iraq, he said, is a "great threat to the United States," and Saddam Hussein has "publicly proclaimed his hatred for our country."

Saddam has used weapons of mass destruction, has defied U.N. resolu-

tions that he disarm and, most recently, "did not even attempt to submit a credible declaration" to the United Nations on his alleged stockpiles of weapons and his programs to develop more.

"If force becomes necessary to secure our country and to keep the peace, America will act deliberately, America will act decisively and America will prevail, because we've got the finest military in the world," Bush said.

The crowd erupted in a deafening cry, "Hoo-ah!"

Bush devoted a single sentence to North Korea, another country he has branded part of an "axis of evil," and one the United States says is now trying to build "mere nuclear weapons.

"In the case of North Korea, the world must continue to speak with one voice to turn that regime away from its nuclear ambitions," he said.

See BUSH/Page 3A

Ohio history lost with time, neglect

PORTLAND (AP) — It was at this tiny river village that the Civil War came to Ohio.

On the morning of July 19, 1863, Union troops waged a four-hour running battle on a foggy Ohio River bend against Confederate Gen. John Morgan, who had cut a swath of destruction through Kentucky, Indiana and Ohio.

Today, the state's only Civil War battlefield is as ghostly as the battle itself, with little to designate its historic significance.

Farmhouses and trailers dot the rolling southeast Ohio bottom land that makes up against the river. A four-acre park with a cobblestone monument and green weathered bronze plaque mark the 1,500-acre battlefield known as Buffington Island. Nearby are a shelter, picnic tables, a lone water pump and a few rusting grills and trash cans.

A gravel company is poised to excavate some of the battlefield,

"I'm just sick, said Keith Ashley, a member of the Ohio Department of Sons of Union Veterans. "I'm seeing history destroyed."

Civil War sites, Underground Railroad stops, pioneer settlements, cemeteries, farmsteads, school buildings and even towns have vanished or are in danger of disappearing as Ohio prepares to celebrate its bicentennial. Neglect, lack of financing and outright disregard have been to blame, historians say.

"We just lose a part of us," said author Randy McNutt, who has written about Ohio and its history.

Housing and commercial developments have carved up some sites. Many historical structures are crumbling.

State Sen. Michael Shoemaker, a Bourneville Democrat, said little government money is available to preserve Ohio's historical sites.

named by the Washington-based Civil War Preservation Trust as among the nation's top 25 most endangered Civil War battlefields.

See HERITAGE/Page 2A

Historian Keith Ashley stands atop an Indian mound overlooking the Buffington Island State Memorial on Dec. 10 near Portland. The memorial stands where Union soldiers battled Confederate troops led by Brig. Gen. John Morgan on July 19, 1863, in the Civil War.

Ohio's heritage

As Ohio prepares to celebrate its 200th year of statehood, pieces of Ohio's heritage have been lost or are in danger of vanishing. The Associated Press has identified and profiled some of the most notable sites and the results are presented in a five-part series:

Part One: History lost to time, neglect. Also, many small museums able to weather tough times.

Part Two: Hidden cemeteries are link to Ohio's settlers. Also, American Indian mounds have been lost with growth.

Part Three: Lands are being restored after generations of use, abuse.

Part Four: Ohio's bleak history fading from landscape.

Part Five: A quiz that takes a fun look at Ohio history.

News Journal
One of Life's Necessities

SATURDAY, JANUARY 4, 2003 — www.mansfieldnewsjournal.com — MANSFIELD, OHIO 50 cents

OSU breaks 'Canes

Buckeyes erupt in celebration after upsetting Miami

Mike Lopresti
Gannett News Service

Move over, Woody. You've never seen anything like it.

Ohio State, a college football hotbed starving 34 years for fulfillment, charged back among the very elite Friday night, stunning No. 1 Miami, 31-24 in two overtimes to capture an unlikely and unforgettable national title.

Miami's 34-game winning streak came crashing down in the first overtime game in BCS history — the long, long night not settled until Ken Dorsey's fourth-down pass from the 1 wobbled into oblivion, the throw made by a quarterback with a hurting shoulder, hurried by the last of a nightful of great Ohio Buckeye defensive plays.

The winning score was Maurice Clarett's 5-yard touchdown run in the second overtime. It was the decisive moment in the game that would not end.

To win its first championship since the Woody Hayes era of 1968 ... to stun the 13-point favorite Hurricanes ... to reverse recent college football history, Ohio State had to first seemingly win the game, then appear to lose it twice.

The Buckeyes were seconds away from the title in regulation, until Todd Sievers' 40-yard field goal as time ran out tied it for Miami.

In the first overtime, Ohio State was down 24-17 and seemed finished when it was fourth down and 14 at its own 29.

But wait. Craig Krenzel's 17-yard pass to Michael Jenkins kept the Buckeyes alive.

"That's the way it's been all year for us ... we've made plays in close games when we've had to," Krenzel said.

Then, Ohio State seemed finished again, for good, when Krenzel's fourth-down pass to Chris Gamble fell away. Firework's were off. The Hurricanes ran onto the field and celebrated.

But wait. There was a late yellow flag. Pass interference on Glenn Sharpe. Krenzel's 1-yard touchdown dive, the 10th play of an exhausting overtime possession, tied it. The

See OSU,
back page

The Buckeyes flood onto the field after defeating the Miami Hurricanes 31-24 in double overtime Friday at the Fiesta Bowl. The victory gave Ohio State their first national championship since 1968. *(Jason J. Molyet/News Journal)*

Buckeye nation filled with joy

Barbara Secrest and Wayne Sutter, both of Shelby, cheer the Buckeyes.

"We both love to follow the Bucks. Win or lose, I won't be disappointed."
— Darrell Secrest
Buckeye fan

News Journal
staff report

Whether it was in a ski lodge south of Mansfield or a tavern in Ashland, area fans came out in droves Friday night to cheer on the Ohio State Buckeyes as they played for college football's national championship.

Their support paid off, as OSU beat the University of Miami in thrilling fashion, 31-24 in double overtime.

A cannon could have been fired down the slopes of Snow Trails without hitting anyone as fans packed the lodge for the kickoff between OSU and the University of Miami.

Mickie Chelski, 46, arrived wearing a Buckeye necklace, with Allison Chelski, 7, and friend Nichole Dragos, 7, in tow.

"This is the second party tonight," Chelski said of the girls. "I was raised a Buckeye, and (Allison's) definitely been raised a Buckeye. They have to win because I said they would."

Scott Gilbert, 47, of Mansfield played football for Otterbein College and has been a Buckeyes' fan all his life. Gilbert predicted a Buckeyes' win by a field goal.

"Coach (Jim) Tressel has turned the whole program around," Gilbert said. "Just the way he disciplines the players and his coaching ability" have led to success.

Cindy Loomis, 45, of Mansfield braved the party in a Miami Hurricanes sweatshirt. She stood outside on the deck but said she hadn't been thrown out.

"I am a Miami fan, and Miami's going to win," Loomis said. "If it were anybody else, I'd be rooting for Ohio State, but since it's Miami — go Miami."

Meanwhile, firefighters at Mansfield's main fire station had everything at their playoff party except alcohol. The eight guys working through the night were watching the game on a large television and feasting on barbecued chicken wings, lunch meat, cheese and chips.

"Miami is going to make

See JOY,
back page

Buckeye fans at Snow Trails react to a play Friday during the Fiesta Bowl. *(Mitchell P. Masilun/News Journal photos)*

A Gannett newspaper

Steelworkers waiting to begin work at AK

By David Benson
News Journal

MANSFIELD — The end of the lockout at AK Steel Corp.'s Mansfield facility may be last year's news, but no union members have entered the mill's gates yet.

"We expect the first 21 to get back there on the 13th of this month, but we still haven't gotten a timetable (from AK Steel) on the rest of our members," United Steelworkers of America Local 169 President Randy Reeder said Friday.

When the company announced the end of the more than three-year lockout Dec. 10 it also sent out recall letters to 27 union date by a week, citing time requirements for medical tests of the workers as a primary reason.

"They also said we requested an extension so (the workers) could give two-week notice to their current employers," Reeder said. "But all we did was ask about it. Some of them don't have jobs, so it wouldn't make sense to make (the notice period) an issue."

Of the original 27 recalled, two have medical issues preventing their immediate return and four have retired. AK Steel has recalled an additional seven union workers who will take their medical exams next week. The slow recall rate concerns the union.

"We need them to call back 50 or 60 at a time. If they just call them back a handful at a time, it'll take forever," Reeder said. "They need to ramp up."

Reeder said his relationship with his AK Steel contact, manager of industrial relations Jack Johnston, is generally good.

"He seems like someone you can discuss things with," Reeder said. "We have a cordial relationship, but we disagree on some issues, sometimes strongly."

Reeder said there was still a lot of doubt among Local 169 members about the eventual outcome of the recall.

"There's a lot of uncertainty — that's the biggest thing. We still don't know the timetable or what conditions they'll find when they get back in there," he said. "I guess I'd say there's both optimism and pessimism about the whole thing. People just want to get their lives back."

The union hall's parking lot was full of cars Friday morning as members came in to get their weekly benefits.

"The biggest misconception people have is that we're all back in the mill," Reeder said. "But the truth is no one is getting paid, and there's no insurance for the members and their families. There's no real difference so far."

Local 169 union members sit at the south gate of the AK Steel Corp. plant in Mansfield. It's been almost a month since AK announced it would bring Steelworkers back to work, but they have yet to enter the plant. *(Daniel Melograna/News Journal)*

maintenance and line workers. The restart date was Monday. But the company has postponed the

---

Special Souvenir
News Journal
One of Life's Necessities

Friday January 3, 2003 — www.mansfieldnewsjournal.com — MANSFIELD, OHIO 50 cents

VICTORY!

Buckeyes Win National Title

- Ohio State fans had already waited 34 years for an undisputed national championship. Certainly Buckeye Nation could hold its collective breath for a couple of nerve-wracking overtime periods in the Fiesta Bowl. See page 1C.

- Their numbers weren't very pretty, but this is one of those times when the statistics lied about the role Ohio State quarterback Craig Krenzel and tailback Maurice Clarett played in delivering a national championship to the Buckeyes. See page 5C.

- Photo page of Buckeyes' win. See page 8C.

- After a week of talk about speed, Ohio State's shot at their first national championship since 1968 came down to a play where that element had no meaning. See page 7C.

- Sun Devil Stadium was packed with Buckeye fans, including some from the Mansfield area for Friday night's college football national championship game between Ohio State and Miami. See page 11A.

- With Ohio Stadium empty, the campus quiet and the Buckeyes playing nearly 1,700 miles away, the city still had a game-day atmosphere. See page 11A.

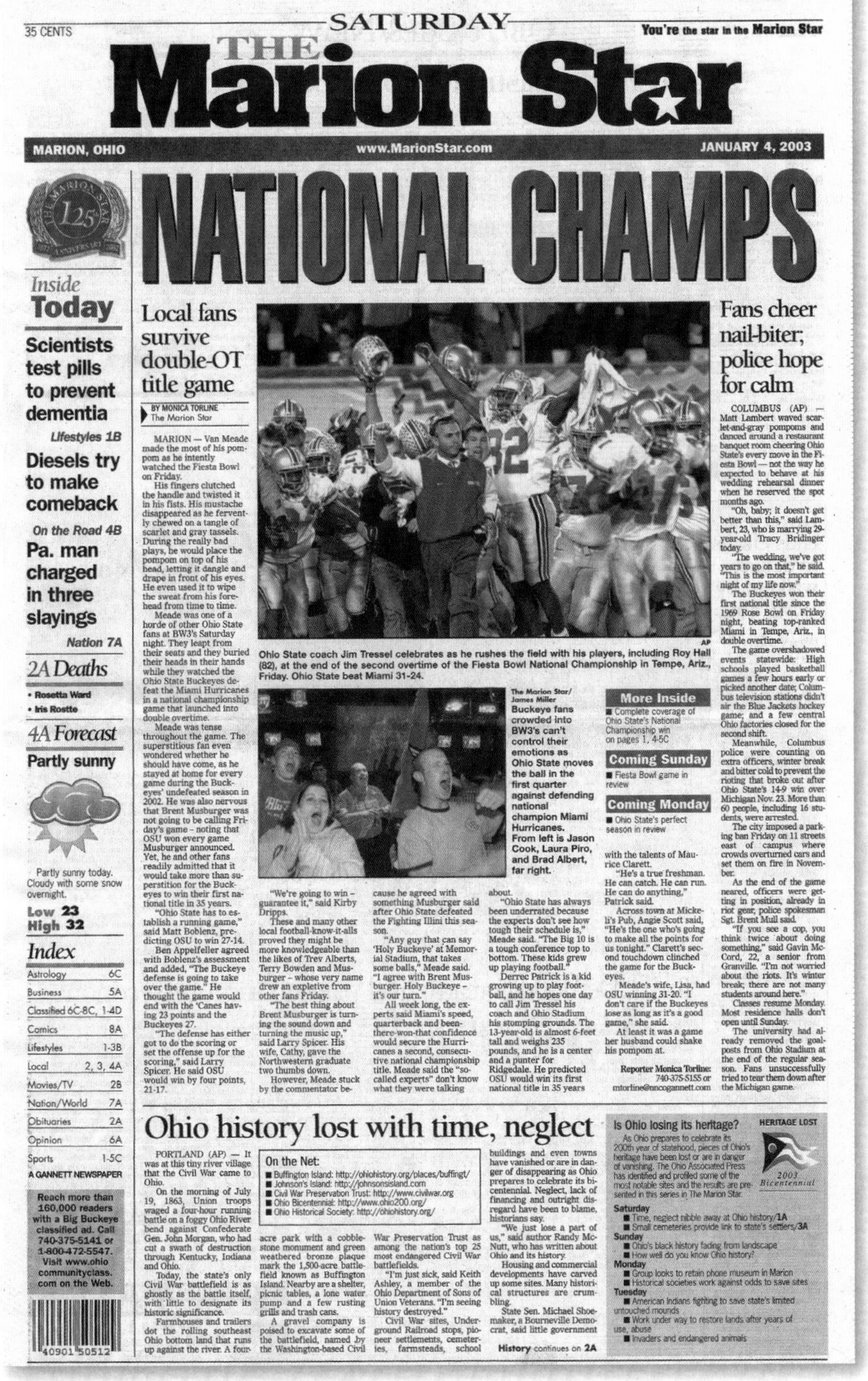

35 CENTS

SATURDAY

THE Marion Star

You're the star in the Marion Star

MARION, OHIO | www.MarionStar.com | JANUARY 4, 2003

125 The Marion Star Anniversary

NATIONAL CHAMPS

Inside Today

Scientists test pills to prevent dementia
Lifestyles 1B

Diesels try to make comeback
On the Road 4B

Pa. man charged in three slayings
Nation 7A

2A Deaths
- Rosetta Ward
- Iris Rostte

4A Forecast

Partly sunny

Partly sunny today. Cloudy with some snow overnight.

Low 23
High 32

Index

Astrology	6C
Business	5A
Classified 6C-8C, 1-4D	
Comics	8A
Lifestyles	1-3B
Local	2, 3, 4A
Movies/TV	2B
Nation/World	7A
Obituaries	2A
Opinion	6A
Sports	1-5C

A GANNETT NEWSPAPER

Reach more than 160,000 readers with a Big Buckeye classified ad. Call 740-375-5141 or 1-800-472-5547. Visit www.ohiocommunityclass.com on the Web.

40901 50512

Local fans survive double-OT title game

BY MONICA TORLINE
The Marion Star

MARION — Van Meade made the most of his pompom as he intently watched the Fiesta Bowl on Friday.

His fingers clutched the handle and twisted it in his fists. His mustache disappeared as he fervently chewed on a tangle of scarlet and gray tassels. During the really bad plays, he would place the pompom on top of his head, letting it dangle and drape in front of his eyes. He even used it to wipe the sweat from his forehead from time to time.

Meade was one of a horde of other Ohio State fans at BW3's Saturday night. They leapt from their seats and they buried their heads in their hands while they watched the Ohio State Buckeyes defeat the Miami Hurricanes in a national championship game that launched into double overtime.

Meade was tense throughout the game. The superstitious fan even wondered whether he should have come, as he stayed at home for every game during the Buckeyes' undefeated season in 2002. He was also nervous that Brent Musburger was not going to be calling Friday's game – noting that OSU won every game Musburger announced. Yet, he and other fans readily admitted that it would take more than superstition for the Buckeyes to win their first national title in 35 years.

"Ohio State has to establish a running game," said Matt Boblenz, predicting OSU to win 27-14.

Ben Appelfeller agreed with Boblenz's assessment and added, "The Buckeye defense is going to take over the game." He thought the game would end with the 'Canes having 23 points and the Buckeyes 27.

"The defense has either got to do the scoring or set the offense up for the scoring," said Larry Spicer. He said OSU would win by four points, 21-17.

"We're going to win – guarantee it," said Kirby Dripps.

These and many other local football-know-it-alls proved they might be more knowledgeable than the likes of Trev Alberts, Terry Bowden and Musburger – whose very name drew an expletive from other fans Friday.

"The best thing about Brent Musburger is turning the sound down and turning the music up," said Larry Spicer. His wife, Cathy, gave the Northwestern graduate two thumbs down.

However, Meade stuck by the commentator because he agreed with something Musburger said after Ohio State defeated the Fighting Illini this season.

"Any guy that can say 'Holy Buckeye' at Memorial Stadium, that takes some balls," Meade said. "I agree with Brent Musburger. Holy Buckeye – it's our turn."

All week long, the experts said Miami's speed, quarterback and been-there-won-that confidence would secure the Hurricanes a second, consecutive national championship title. Meade said the "so-called experts" don't know what they were talking about.

"Ohio State has always been underrated because the experts don't see how tough their schedule is," Meade said. "The Big 10 is a tough conference top to bottom. These kids grew up playing football."

Derrec Patrick is a kid growing up to play football, and he hopes one day to call Jim Tressel his coach and Ohio Stadium his stomping grounds. The 13-year-old is almost 6-feet tall and weighs 235 pounds, and he is a center and a punter for Ridgedale. He predicted OSU would win its first national title in 35 years with the talents of Maurice Clarett.

"He's a true freshman. He can catch. He can run. He can do anything," Patrick said.

Across town at Mickeli's Pub, Angie Scott said, "He's the one who's going to make all the points for us tonight." Clarett's second touchdown clinched the game for the Buckeyes.

Meade's wife, Lisa, had OSU winning 31-20. "I don't care if the Buckeyes lose as long as it's a good game," she said.

At least it was a game her husband could shake his pompom at.

Reporter Monica Torline: 740-375-5155 or mtorline@nncogannett.com

AP

Ohio State coach Jim Tressel celebrates as he rushes the field with his players, including Roy Hall (82), at the end of the second overtime of the Fiesta Bowl National Championship in Tempe, Ariz., Friday. Ohio State beat Miami 31-24.

The Marion Star/James Miller

Buckeye fans crowded into BW3's can't control their emotions as Ohio State moves the ball in the first quarter against defending national champion Miami Hurricanes. From left is Jason Cook, Laura Piro, and Brad Albert, far right.

More Inside
- Complete coverage of Ohio State's National Championship win on pages 1, 4-5C

Coming Sunday
- Fiesta Bowl game in review

Coming Monday
- Ohio State's perfect season in review

Fans cheer nail-biter; police hope for calm

COLUMBUS (AP) — Matt Lambert waved scarlet-and-gray pompoms and danced around a restaurant banquet room cheering Ohio State's every move in the Fiesta Bowl — not the way he expected to behave at his wedding rehearsal dinner when he reserved the spot months ago.

"Oh, baby; it doesn't get better than this," said Lambert, 23, who is marrying 29-year-old Tracy Bridinger today.

"The wedding, we've got years to go on that," he said. "This is the most important night of my life now."

The Buckeyes won their first national title since the 1969 Rose Bowl on Friday night, beating top-ranked Miami in Tempe, Ariz., in double overtime.

The game overshadowed events statewide: High schools played basketball games a few hours early or picked another date; Columbus television stations didn't air the Blue Jackets hockey game; and a few central Ohio factories closed for the second shift.

Meanwhile, Columbus police were counting on extra officers, winter break and bitter cold to prevent the rioting that broke out after Ohio State's 14-9 win over Michigan Nov. 23. More than 60 people, including 16 students, were arrested.

The city imposed a parking ban Friday on 11 streets east of campus where crowds overturned cars and set them on fire in November.

As the end of the game neared, officers were getting in position, already in riot gear, police spokesman Sgt. Brent Mull said.

"If you see a cop, you think twice about doing something," said Gavin McCord, 22, a senior from Granville. "I'm not worried about the riots. It's winter break; there are not many students around here."

Classes resume Monday. Most residence halls don't open until Sunday.

The university had already removed the goalposts from Ohio Stadium at the end of the regular season. Fans unsuccessfully tried to tear them down after the Michigan game.

Ohio history lost with time, neglect

PORTLAND (AP) — It was at this tiny river village that the Civil War came to Ohio.

On the morning of July 19, 1863, Union troops waged a four-hour running battle on a foggy Ohio River bend against Confederate Gen. John Morgan, who had cut a swath of destruction through Kentucky, Indiana and Ohio.

Today, the state's only Civil War battlefield is as ghostly as the battle itself, with little to designate its historic significance.

Farmhouses and trailers dot the rolling southeast Ohio bottom land that runs up against the river. A four-acre park with a cobblestone monument and green weathered bronze plaque mark the 1,500-acre battlefield known as Buffington Island. Nearby are a shelter, picnic tables, a lone water pump and a few rusting grills and trash cans.

A gravel company is poised to excavate some of the battlefield, named by the Washington-based Civil War Preservation Trust as among the nation's top 25 most endangered Civil War battlefields.

"I'm just sick, said Keith Ashley, a member of the Ohio Department of Sons of Union Veterans. "I'm seeing history destroyed."

Civil War sites, Underground Railroad stops, pioneer settlements, cemeteries, farmsteads, school buildings and even towns have vanished or are in danger of disappearing as Ohio prepares to celebrate its bicentennial. Neglect, lack of financing and outright disregard have been to blame, historians say.

"We just lose a part of us," said author Randy McNutt, who has written about Ohio and its history.

Housing and commercial developments have carved up some sites. Many historical structures are crumbling.

State Sen. Michael Shoemaker, a Bourneville Democrat, said little government

History continues on 2A

On the Net:
- Buffington Island: http://ohiohistory.org/places/buffingt/
- Johnson's Island: http://johnsonsisland.com
- Civil War Preservation Trust: http://www.civilwar.org
- Ohio Bicentennial: http://www.ohio200.org/
- Ohio Historical Society: http://ohiohistory.org/

Is Ohio losing its heritage?

HERITAGE LOST
2003 Bicentennial

As Ohio prepares to celebrate its 200th year of statehood, pieces of Ohio's heritage have been lost or are in danger of vanishing. The Ohio Associated Press has identified and profiled some of the most notable sites and the results are presented in this series in The Marion Star.

Saturday
- Time, neglect nibble away at Ohio history/1A
- Small cemeteries provide link to state's settlers/3A

Sunday
- Ohio's black history fading from landscape
- How well do you know Ohio history?

Monday
- Group looks to retain phone museum in Marion
- Historical societies work against odds to save sites

Tuesday
- American Indians fighting to save state's limited untouched mounds
- Work under way to restore lands after years of use, abuse
- Invaders and endangered animals

INSIDE: D.M. Ford family files wrongful death lawsuit, Page 4A.

Serving Zanesville and Southeastern Ohio since 1852

TIMES RECORDER

Today: Cloudy
High near 32
Details on Page 6A

A Gannett Newspaper | Saturday, Jan. 4, 2003 | 35¢

CHAMPIONS!

Buckeyes capture unforgettable title over Hurricanes

By MIKE LOPRESTI
Gannett News Service

TEMPE, Ariz. — Move over, Woody. You've never seen anything like it

Ohio State, a college football hotbed starving 34 years for fulfillment, charged back among the very elite Friday night, stunning No. 1 Miami, 31-24 in two overtimes to capture an unlikely and unforgettable national title.

Miami's 34-game winning streak came crashing down in the first overtime game in BCS history - the long, long night not settled until Ken Dorsey's fourth down pass from the 1 wobbled into oblivion, the throw made by a quarterback with a hurting shoulder, hurried by the last of a nightful of great Ohio Buckeye defensive plays.

The winning score was Maurice Clarett's five-yard touchdown run in the second overtime. It was the decisive moment in the game that would not end.

To win its first championship since the Woody Hayes era of 1968 ... to stun the 13-point favorite Hurricanes ... to reverse recent college football history, Ohio State had to first seemingly win the game, then appear to lose it twice.

The Buckeyes were seconds away from the title in regulation, until Todd Sievers' 40-yard field goal as time ran out tied it for Miami, this from a man who had not ... one in nearly two months.

In the first overtime, Ohio State was down 24-17 and seemed finished when it was fourth down and 14 at its own 29.

But wait. Craig Krenzel's 17-yard pass to Michael Jenkins kept the Buckeyes alive.

"That's the way it's been all year for us ... we've made plays in close games when we've had to," Krenzel said.

Then, Ohio State seemed finished again, for good, when Krenzel's fourth down pass to Chris Gamble fell away. Fireworks went off. The Hurricanes ran onto the field and celebrated.

But wait. There was a late yellow flag. Pass interference on Glenn Sharpe. Krenzel's 1-yard touchdown dive, the 10th play of an exhausting overtime possession, tied it. The Miami celebration will be a sad footnote for their history.

Even the second overtime almost got away from the 14-0 Buckeyes.

Miami died when it could not score on four plays from the two-yard line.

Quadtrine Hill's run went for a yard. Dorsey missed open tight end Eric Winston. Hill was stopped for no gain. And Dorsey was hurried into a duck by a blitzing Cie Grant.

Where were the Hurricane big-play masters? Hurt. Dorsey had injured his shoulder just minutes before, but played on. Willis McGahee was gone in the fourth with an injured knee.

To win the overtime, Ohio State had to get there the old-fashioned way. The defense wrecked the Hurricanes by strangling their big-name attack and forcing them into five turnovers.

See CHAMPIONS, Page 6A

85503 00460

DANTE SMITH/Times Recorder

Ohio State's Donnie Nickey holds up the Fiesta Bowl trophy after the Buckeyes defeated Miami to become the National Champions.

Buckeye fans, from left, Matt Howell, Kevin Brown, Mike King and Stephanie King celebrate the Buckeyes' second touchdown as Miami fan Terra Hindel, background, watches during the Fiesta Bowl Friday night at the King household in Nashport.

CHRIS CROOK/Times Recorder

Screams, prayers, hugs for local fans

By DAVE WEIDIG
TR Sports Editor

ZANESVILLE — Jim Burkhart kept rubbing his lucky piece of goalpost throughout the game.

Evidently, it paid off.

He had secured his prized possession at Ohio State's last national championship win, in the 1969 Rose Bowl, and at about 12:30 a.m. today, he got to celebrate another.

This one came at the Knights Of Columbus Hall after the Buckeyes pulled out a dramatic 31-24 double-overtime win over No. 1 Miami in the Fiesta Bowl.

"I'm mad I wasn't there; I should have been there. I have a brother and sister out there," he said.

Tony Hutcheson of Zanesville and his family were there, but weren't able to obtain tickets until Friday afternoon. They paid $725 apiece, but it was worth it. They sat in a sea of Ohio State fans, in the second row of the end zone.

"It's one of the best football games I've ever seen, at any level," he said as he left Sun Devil Stadium. "I'm so excited, I don't know what to say. I just thank God my family and I had this opportunity. We'll remember it the rest of our lives."

See FANS, Page 6A

Work didn't keep some from watching Ohio State history

By DEVIN SHULTZ
TR Sports Writer

ZANESVILLE — Some people stayed home to watch the Ohio State-Miami national championship game Friday night. Others went to a party. Some stuck with option three: Work.

But not even that could stop area fans from enjoying the biggest OSU game since the national title in 1968, one that ended with a thrilling 31-24 double-overtime win over the heavily-favored Hurricanes.

John Fisk of the Zanesville Fire Department was lucky enough to get the evening off. But his co-workers held down the fort and watched the game, "even though they're not the biggest fans..." Fisk said.

Fisk was prepared — if he had to work late. "In case I had to stay over, I brought a walkman with me, so I could keep a bug in my ear as I went on a run," he said.

Pizza drivers had a busy Friday night, but that didn't stop them from getting the latest score. Mark King, general manager of Domino's South, said the radio would be his team's best friend.

"We have no cable access, so we can't watch the game," King said. But, he added, drivers were able to sneak a peek, "while delivering pizza to a customer's house."

King said Domino's South would probably make between $500 to $1,000 extra, because of the game.

Mary Jane O'Hare's grandson, OSU senior Marshall Altier, was in Arizona for the game. But she was behind the control desk at Maysville All-Star Lanes. She didn't mind much, since the bowling score monitors were broadcasting the game.

"We decided to have open bowling for $1.50 a game, which is unusual," O'Hare added. "We usually have a league on Friday nights, but they decided not to bowl because of the game."

Being able to mingle with OSU fans at the bowling alley made watching the Fiesta Bowl that much better for O'Hare.

"I enjoy it here because there are more people to enjoy the game with," O'Hare said. "It's a lot better than sitting at home."

dshultz@nncogannett.com
450-6761

Left Newspaper — News Herald

Upgrade on schedule
Old jailhouse being revamped for offices.
Local, A3

Pakistanis protest against U.S-Iraq war
Hard-line Islamic leaders called for Friday demonstrations across country.
Nation/World, A5

Redskins beat Rockets
Turnovers hurt Oak Harbor in 61-47 loss to Port Clinton.
Sports, B1

News Herald

Port Clinton, Ohio   www.portclintonnewsherald.com   50¢

Saturday
Jan. 4, 2003

Weather
High 30s
Waves 1-3 feet
Winds 10-25 knots
Details, A2

Associated Press
Danielle van Dam

Girl's killer gets death sentence
Associated Press

SAN DIEGO — The man who kidnapped and murdered 7-year-old neighbor Danielle van Dam was sentenced to death Friday after the little girl's sobbing mother branded him a "monster" deserving of no mercy.

David Westerfield showed no emotion as a judge imposed the sentence a jury had recommended in September. The 50-year-old engineer declined to make a statement, turning aside the mother's plea for an apology.

Danielle was snatched from her bedroom last February in the first in a string of child abductions that gripped the nation last year.

Prosecutors said there was no justification for anything less than the death penalty for such an "evil, selfish, cold-hearted child killer."

Deaths
Ruth M. Horrelbrink
Elmore
Daniel N. Hockett
Oak Harbor
Robert W. Franck
Oak Harbor
– Details, A3

Lottery
Pick 3: 6-0-0
Pick 4: 7-5-1-5X
Buckeye 5: 4-19-23-29-33
DAY DRAWINGS
Pick 3: 3-4-9
Pick 4: 4-4-2-2
Mega Millions: 6-14-28-37-46
Mega Ball: 3

Call us
For news, sports, advertising or home delivery:
News: 419-734-7903
Sports: 419-734-7519
Circulation customer service: 419-734-7525
Classified advertising: 419-734-7512
Other departments: 419-734-7500
Toll Free: (800) 636-6906

Index
Annie's M'box   A6   Business   A8
Nation/World   A5   Obituaries   A3
Classified   A6-7   Sports   B1-4
Comics   A7   Stocks   A8
Editorial   A4   Weather   A2
Kathy Sump   A3

A Gannett Newspaper
GANNETT
Printed on recycled paper.
Copyright 2003

Fiesta Bowl 2003
Buckeyes win!
OSU 31
Miami 24
Associated Press

TEMPE, Ariz. — Perfectly shocking! Perfectly thrilling!

Ohio State worked two overtimes to rip the national championship from the confident 'Canes.

Now the Buckeyes are the best.

Maurice Clarett ran 6 yards for the winning touchdown, and Ohio State's defense turned back one final Miami bid to tie the game. With that, the Buckeyes completed an unlikely, unbeaten run to their first national title in 34 years with a 31-24 win Friday night at the Fiesta Bowl.

The Buckeyes' upset ended the Hurricanes' bid for a second straight title and their winning streak at 34 in one of college football's greatest games ever.

But it would have never happened if not for a late pass interference call at the end of the first overtime — which came with Miami players already celebrating an apparent championship.

Instead, the fourth-down call gave Ohio State the chance it needed to tie the game and send it into the second overtime.

News Herald/ABIGAIL BOBROW
Brothers David and Dennison Sparks, both of Port Clinton, celebrate during the OSU/Miami game at Bell Mell Tavern.

Fans hail National Champions
By RICK NEALE
Staff writer

PORT CLINTON — It was one of the classic college football games in history, and bedlam reigned inside Bell Mell Tavern.

Buckeye fans packed every nook and cranny of the Fulton Street bar during Friday's Fiesta Bowl, glued to television screens during Ohio State's 31-24 double-overtime cliffhanger win over mighty Miami.

"It's always been a Buckeye bar," Port Clinton resident Randy Miller Jr. said. "My grandpa came in here in the '60s for the Ohio State-Michigan games."

For the Miller family,

And they barely avoided heart attacks. Fans beat on walls and tables, screamed, held hands, prayed and covered their eyes throughout the gut-wrenching fourth quarter and overtime periods.

the Fiesta Bowl added a dramatic chapter to its ongoing Ohio State legacy. Randy Miller III and his father, Miller Jr., fired a noisy scarlet-and-gray bazooka in the air during opening kickoffs, just as they did during last month's OSU-Michigan game.

"My dad built that cannon 25 years ago,"

See ANXIETY, A3

Inside
Details and photos of the game
— B1 and B3
OSU season review
The Ohio State season will be reviewed in a special section. — Monday

Sledding accident reveals hidden dangers
By RICK NEALE
Staff writer

PORT CLINTON — Beware, Portage Park sledders: Danger might be lurking just beneath the show's surface.

Parks and Recreation Director Ken Gipe warns that hidden ramps and obstacles present a safety hazard on Taft Hill. Last week, he said a girl suffered a bruised back after she inadvertently sledded over a snowboarding ramp, then wiped out in violent fashion.

"It's just like skateboarding," Gipe said of sledding. "Believe it or not, it's a dangerous activity."

The ramp mishap occurred Dec. 27. Gipe declined to reveal the identity

of the injured girl, who was about 10 years old.

"It could have been serious, had she landed on her head or something like that," he said.

Gipe blamed a buried, abandoned ramp for the accident.

"Evidently, some kids that use snowboards built a little skateboard ramp and packed it down under the snow," he said. "They were going down the hill and probably doing jumps and turns.

"I know in the past they've built snow ramps, but that's only about a foot high. After you go over that two or three times, it's gone anyway. If they were snowboarding off of it, there would have had to be some

structure to it."

After the girl's spectacular wipe-out, Gipe said a group of parents dug out the ramp and dragged it off Taft Hill.

For safe measure, he said sledders should keep their eyes peeled for obstacles on Taft Hill. He added they should avoid sledding toward the nearby fence.

"Believe it or not, people go down that side. I don't know if they're trying to imitate something from that movie 'Jackass' or something."

To report sledding obstacles at Portage Park, call the parks and recreation department at 732-2200 or the police department at 734-3121.

Sledding safety tips
Nationwide, sledding accidents send more than 95,000 victims to hospital emergency rooms, according to Watson Pediatric Physicians. Here's some easy-to-digest safety hints compiled by the Massachusetts-based organization:
■ Avoid sledding toward fences, trees, rock walls, roads, parking lots, ponds or lakes.
■ Don't use a sled with sharp edges.
■ Avoid crowds of other sledders.
■ Use a helmet.
■ Adult supervision is preferred.

Courts
Judge dismisses felony charge against Else Baumgartner
By JENNIFER FUNK
Staff writer

PORT CLINTON — Instead of facing a felony escape charge, Oak Harbor lawyer and proclaimed whistleblower Elsebeth Baumgartner will likely face a misdemeanor version.

That's after Ottawa County Common Pleas Judge Paul C. Moon dismissed the felony charge Friday on a legal technicality following a contentious hearing.

Special Prosecutor Tim Braun said after the hearing that he would refile the escape charge in Ottawa County Municipal Court as a misdemeanor.

Braun said, too, he considered the misdemeanor charge, but a grand jury chose otherwise.

"I'm not over there when they vote or discuss the case," Braun said of the October grand jury that indicted Baumgartner.

Meanwhile, Baumgartner remains in jail until a 1 p.m. hearing on Thursday in municipal court on a probation violation allegation.

Moon's decision to dismiss the case surprised even Baumgartner's lawyer, Gerald Walton, who argued during the hearing to have both Moon and

Else Baumgartner
■ Judge Paul Moon explains his decision. See Page A2.

Braun step down from the case.

"No, I wasn't anticipating that," Walton said afterward. "I am pleased with it, but I wasn't anticipating that."

At one point during the hearing, Walton asked Moon if his client could speak, but Moon denied the request.

Walton said later he wasn't sure what she wanted to say.

"I'm not sure the totality of what she was going to say," he said. "I'm not so happy that we never got to address several things."

Many of the courtroom's

See JUDGE, A2

Nuclear power industry
Report: NRC kept Davis-Besse plant open despite safety concerns
Associated Press

WASHINGTON — The Nuclear Regulatory Commission could have shut down a Carroll Township nuclear plant several months before an acid leak was discovered but wanted to avoid hurting parent company FirstEnergy financially, according to a report released Friday by the agency's watchdog.

The report, released by the NRC's Office of Inspector General, was at the behest of the Union of Concerned Scientists, a watchdog group in Washington, D.C. concerned about the federal agency's handling of the Davis-Besse Nuclear Power Station situation.

The damage at the local power plant was the most extensive corrosion ever at

a U.S. nuclear reactor.

In the fall of 2001, the NRC identified 12 nuclear power plants as being "highly susceptible" to corrosion and ordered the plants to perform inspections. All but Davis-Besse shut down for inspections by January 2002.

After at least five plants found small cracks, the NRC drafted a letter requiring the 25-year-old Davis-Besse plant to shut down. The agency backed off when plant owner FirstEnergy Corp. said such a shutdown would be costly and could cause wintertime power shortages in northwest Ohio, according to the report.

The report also said top

See REPORT, A3

'Waking Ned Devine' launches film festival Sunday at library
By JENNIFER FUNK
Staff writer

PORT CLINTON — The Friends of Ida Rupp Public Library want to give area residents a movie experience they wouldn't ordinarily have.

So at the behest of another member, the president of the non-profit group, Peggy Debien, decided to launch a film festival for 2003. The program starts Sunday afternoon with a showing of "Waking Ned Devine," a British comedy.

The group will offer microwave popcorn, coffee and pop during the free showing, said Debien.

The Friends of Ida Rupp worked for a year securing a license to be allowed to show recently released-to-video films, and Debien spent hours watching videos and pulling together recommendations from fellow movie buffs.

The movies — from popular foreign titles to obscure critically-acclaimed

See 'WAKING,' A3

What's Playing ...And When
■ Waking Ned Devine — 2 p.m. Sunday.
■ Postino — 2 p.m. Friday, Jan. 10.
■ Indochine — 7 p.m. Friday, Jan. 17.
■ Spiderman — 2 p.m. Saturday, Jan. 26.
■ Iris — 7 p.m. Friday, Jan. 31.
■ My Father's Glory — 7 p.m. Friday, Feb. 7.
■ Amelie — 7 p.m. Friday, Feb. 14.
■ The Color of Paradise — 7 p.m. Friday, Feb. 21.
■ Old Yeller — 2 p.m. Sunday, Feb. 23.
■ Disney's Fantasia — 2 p.m. Sunday, March 1.
■ Babette's Feast — 7 p.m. Friday, March 7.
■ Billy Elliott — 7 p.m. Friday, March 14.
■ Lagaan — 7 p.m. Friday, March 21.
■ My Mother's Castle — 2 p.m. Sunday, March 30.

Right Newspaper — The News-Messenger

HIGH SCHOOL BOYS BASKETBALL SCOREBOARD			MORE IN SPORTS, B1-6
Whitmer 65	Margaretta 57	Old Fort..............94	Lima Senior 67
Ross 76	Clyde 68	Carey 82	Tol. Woodward ..37
SJCC 56	New Riegel 85	Port Clinton 61	Ottawa Hills 51
St. Wendelin 82	Bettsville 52	Oak Harbor 47	Cardinal Stritch 37

The News-Messenger

Fremont, Ohio   www.thenews-messenger.com   Saturday, January 4, 2003   50 Cents

Weather
Today: Mostly cloudy. Highs in the lower 30s.
Sunday: Snow likely. Highs in the lower 30s.
Complete weather: A10

Bucks win!!!

Associated Press file photo
DANIELLE VAN DAM

Van Dam murderer sentenced to death
Associated Press

SAN DIEGO — The man who kidnapped and murdered 7-year-old neighbor Danielle van Dam was sentenced to death Friday after the little girl's sobbing mother branded him a "monster" deserving of no mercy.

David Westerfield showed no emotion as a judge imposed the sentence a jury had recommended in September. The 50-year-old engineer declined to make a statement, turning aside the mother's plea for an apology.

"What were you thinking as you killed her? Did she not touch your heart one bit? If not, you are heartless. You are an empty shell." Danielle's mother, Brenda, said as she fought back tears. "It disgusts me that your sick fantasies and pitiful needs made you think that you needed Danielle more than her family."

Prosecutors said there was no justification for anything less than the death penalty for such an "evil, selfish, cold-hearted child killer."

See JUDGE, A2

WESTERFIELD

Deaths
Robert Franck, Oak Harbor
Daniel Hockett, Oak Harbor
Ruth Horrelbrink, Elmore
Bernice McCarthy, Columbus
Donald Motyel, Fremont
Obituaries, A2

Ohio Lottery
Friday's winners:
Pick 3: 389 (day); 600(night)
Pick 4: 4422 (day); 7538 (night)
Buckeye 5: 4-19-23-29-33
Super Lotto: $15 million
Mega Millions: 6-14-26-37-46
Mega Ball: 3

Inside
Classified B3   Local A3
Comics A9   Nat./World A5
Deaths A2   Records A2
Editorials A4   Sports B1-6
Mktpl.   Weather A10

The News-Messenger is printed on recycled paper.
A Gannett Newspaper
Copyright 2003

Ohio State 31, Miami 24 (2OT)
Associated Press

TEMPE, Ariz. — Perfectly shocking! Perfectly thrilling!

Ohio State worked two overtimes to rip the national championship from the confident 'Canes.

Now the Buckeyes are the best.

Maurice Clarett ran 6 yards for the winning touchdown, and Ohio State's defense turned back one final Miami bid to tie the game. With that, the Buckeyes completed an unlikely, unbeaten run to their first national title in 34 years with a 31-34 win Friday night at the Fiesta Bowl.

The Buckeyes' upset ended the Hurricanes' bid for a second straight title and their winning streak at 34 in one of college football's greatest games ever.

But it would have never happened if not for a late pass interference call at the end of the first overtime — which came with Miami players already celebrating an apparent championship.

Instead, the fourth-down call gave Ohio State the chance it needed to tie the game and send it into the second overtime.

By then, it already was a classic — the national championship game to go into overtime, in a matchup of the nation's last two undefeated teams.

TYRONE STOKES of Port Clinton and Al Weyer of Clyde celebrate Mike Doss's interception in the second quarter of the Fiesta Bowl at Mike & Ninfa's Bar & Grill Friday night.
News-Messenger/Ben French

Fans cheer national champs
By IASHA STAFFORD
Staff writer

John Weiker attributes Ohio State's championship against Miami University to his establishment's new paint job. Weiker, owner of Bud's Tavern, 1720 W. State St., recently painted the outside of the building scarlet and gray, the Buckeyes' school colors, and the front door of Bud's sports an Ohio State University emblem. The paint job led to the title, he said.

"We are taking full credit for their winning streak," Weiker said.

A small crowd gathered inside of the bar to watch the game and enjoy the free food that was provided as part of the Fiesta Bowl festivities.

One man at Bud's took his team spirit as far as wearing Ohio State University pajamas.

Whether fans pledge their allegiance to the Buckeyes by painting their businesses and homes or opt to sport team paraphernalia — the love of the team was present all over Fremont Friday night.

"It's like this every Ohio State game," said Joan Van Ness, owner of Time Out Sports Bar, 2004 Lake St. The bar has been open for more than 10 years.

Her husband and son traveled to Tempe, Ariz., to watch the big game from club seats, while she watched the

See OSU, A10

JON PETERS of Fremont shows his colors prior to the start of the Fiesta Bowl in Tempe, Ariz., Friday.
Associated Press

Inside
Details and photos of the game
— B1 and B3
OSU season review
The Ohio State season will be reviewed in a special section. — Monday

Parents group to meet Monday
Group will focus on financial miseries of Fremont schools
By SARAH WILLIAMS
Staff writer

Hoping to help curb Fremont City Schools' financial misery, parents and community members plan to work with school administrators to try to secure more dollars for the institution.

The group of parents will meet for the first time at 6:30 p.m. Monday at the school administration building on Cedar Street. Community members who would like to contribute ideas are invited to attend.

The group hopes to work closely with Superintendent Don King and the Fremont school board. King said that administrators will begin looking this month at which type of levy they'll want to put on the ballot in May. They will also look at restricting the elementary schools, open enrollment and cuts since the school's levy failed to pass in November.

Voters rejected a 3.9 mill property tax levy that would have generated $2.135 million each year and helped the school break from the need for property tax advances. The school will need to seek another advance, although Treasurer Matt Feasel predicts that without one, the school would end the year about $2.6 million in debt — without making cuts.

Parent group organizer Tim Ellenberger suggested at the school board's December meeting that the board work with him and the parent group to conduct focus groups, answer community questions and better inform the public of the school's situation.

As the group continues to meet, Ellenberger said the fate of the following district services will be up for discussion at the meeting:
■ Academic programs, including honors, advanced placement and post-secondary options offerings;
■ Art, music and physical education in the elementary schools;
■ Clubs, sports, busing and other transportation;

The group will also look for information regarding the effects of elementary school redistricting and the possibility of open enrollment.

Contact staff writer Sarah Williams at 419-334-1051 or swilliam@fremont.gannett.com

If you go
Anyone with questions or suggestions about Fremont City Schools' financial situation or the pending levy for the May election can attend a meeting Monday, made up of parents and community members.

The meeting will be held at 6:30 p.m. in the lecture room of the school administration building on Cedar Street.

NRC's concern for owner's financial straits kept D-B plant open, watchdog report says
Associated Press

WASHINGTON — The Nuclear Regulatory Commission could have shut down a Carroll Township nuclear plant several months before an acid leak was discovered but wanted to avoid hurting parent company FirstEnergy financially, according to a report released Friday by the agency's watchdog.

The report, released by

the NRC's Office of Inspector General, was at the behest of the Union of Concerned Scientists, a watchdog group in Washington, D.C. concerned about the federal agency's handling of the Davis-Besse Nuclear Power Station situation.

The damage at the local power plant was the most extensive corrosion ever at a U.S. nuclear reactor.

In the fall of 2001, the

NRC identified 12 nuclear power plants as being "highly susceptible" to corrosion and ordered the plants to perform inspections. All but Davis-Besse shut down for inspections by January 2002.

After at least five plants found small cracks, the NRC drafted a letter requiring the 25-year-old Davis-Besse plant to shut down. The agency backed off when

plant owner FirstEnergy Corp. said such a shutdown would be costly and could cause wintertime power shortages in northwest Ohio, according to the report.

The report also said top agency safety officials had strong justification to order Davis-Besse shut down earlier but instead allowed FirstEnergy to continue making energy at the plant

See FINANCIAL, A10

LANCASTER EAGLE-GAZETTE

Saturday

January 4, 2003

YOUR NEWS. YOUR PAPER.

First of the year
First New Year baby at FMC finally arrives
PAGE 3A

Significant match-up
Lancaster boys set for showdown with Newark
PAGE 3B

Friday Scores
BOYS BASKETBALL
■ Pickerington 50, Westerville N. 42
GIRLS BASKETBALL
■ Millersport 48, Licking Heights 44
■ Heath 63, Liberty Union 47
Details in Section B

Serving Fairfield County — A Gannett Newspaper — 35 cents ■ 24 pages

Champions!

OSU wins first title since 1968

By JON SPENCER
Gannett News Service

TEMPE, Ariz. — Ohio State fans had already waited 34 years for an undisputed national championship. Certainly Buckeye Nation could hold its collective breath for a couple of nerve-wracking overtime periods in the Fiesta Bowl.

Coming back from the brink with two fourth-down conversions in the first OT, the Buckeyes rode Maurice Clarett's five-yard run and an ensuing goal-line stand to Friday night's 31-24 double-overtime victory over the Miami Hurricanes in Sun Devil Stadium.

Bush: 'We're ready'
President Bush tells troops to prepare for military action.
PAGE 6A

Gas prices to increase
Columbia Gas announced an increase in gas rates for its customers.
PAGE 3A

Protest continues
West Virginia surgeons remain on strike to protest medical malpractice insurance costs.
PAGE 5A

Coming Up
Car insurance rates are skyrocketing; insurance providers point to several factors.
Sunday

Weather
Today will be mostly cloudy.
High: 32   Low: 27
Details on page 2A

Jim Tressel and the Ohio State Buckeyes celebrate after the team's 31-24 defeat in double overtime of the University of Miami in the Fiesta Bowl on Friday in Tempe, Ariz. Ohio State won its first national title since 1968. (GNS photo by Jason J. Molyet)

Inside:
■ Game analysis, page 1B.
■ Fans represent Ohio in Tempe, page 1B.
■ Buckeyes best in the land, page 1B.
■ Defense came through, page 6B.
■ More from the game, page 6B.
■ OSU photo spread, page 7B.
■ Coming up Monday: Special OSU section.

Fans speechless after wild win

By CARRIE BOLSEN
The Eagle-Gazette Staff

Working doesn't keep people from watching

By HOLLIE SAUNDERS
The Eagle-Gazette Staff

Arson charges reinstated

By KRISTIN GORDON
The Eagle-Gazette Staff

Teen rape suspect will be tried as adult

By KRISTIN GORDON
The Eagle-Gazette Staff

Index
Advice	7A
Classified	8B-11B
Comics	12B
Legal Notices	11B
Obituaries	5A
Opinion	4A
Religion	8A-9A
Television	10A

COSHOCTON TRIBUNE
A REFLECTION OF HOME.

Saturday
Jan. 4, 2003

A Gannett Newspaper — www.coshoctontribune.com — 35¢

Tonight: Cloudy Low near 22
Sunday: Snow High near 35
Details on Page 4A

31 Ohio State — Miami 24

A Buckeye breath-holder

National Champion OSU takes win in double overtime

Ianniello's BP employee Jen Scherer works alongside her radio. Many Buckeye fans tuned into the Fiesta Bowl while working their second shift jobs.
TREVOR JONES/Tribune

Miss the game? Not a chance

Workers stay glued to radio, television wherever possible

By ROBIN EAVES
Tribune Staff Writer

COSHOCTON — Jimmy McClure was one of several area residents depending on the Voice of Buckeyes, Paul Keals, to keep him updated on the national championship game Friday.

"I couldn't watch the game, but I at least wanted to hear it."
— Jimmy McClure, who works second shift at Annin Flag Company.

Andrews

Ford

Garvin

McClure

Parks

Ohio State's Maurice Clarett dives into the end zone during the second overtime of Friday's Fiesta Bowl game.
Photos by DANTE SMITH/Tribune

Ohio State caps perfect season with win over Hurricanes

By MIKE LOPRESTI
Gannett News Service

TEMPE, Ariz. — Move over, Woody. You've never seen anything like it.

Ohio State, a college football hotbed starving 34 years for fulfillment, charged back among the very elite Friday night, stunning No. 1 Miami, 31-24 in two overtimes to capture an unlikely and unforgettable national title.

Ohio State fans celebrate the Buckeyes first touchdown of the game Friday at the Fiesta Bowl.

See SEASON, Page 4A

Buckeye fans (and a loyal Wolverine) gather for the big game

By JIM BARSTOW
Tribune Sports Editor

FRESNO — When a garage full of 21 people transformed into a mosh pit, one got an indication that something good had finally happened for Apalachin Ohio.

■ Inside
Fiesta Bowl game story
See page 1B

Ohio State fills seats at Fiesta Bowl
Gannett News Service

TEMPE, Ariz — Nebraska's vaunted sea of red has nothing on Ohio State.

See LOCAL FANS, Page 3A

Buckeye fans unrivaled

Buckeye fans are unrivaled in the support they give their team.

From the sellouts at Ohio Stadium, where more than 105,000 pack the Horseshoe, to the support they give on the road to the incredible turnout at the Fiesta Bowl, there's no denying the intensity with which they support the scarlet and gray.

Buckeye fans filling Sun Devil Stadium in Tempe, Ariz., when Ohio State played Miami for the national championship outnumbered Hurricane fans four to one. Coach Jim Tressel said it felt like a home game.

Here is a look at some of the Ohio State fans from the 2002 season.

Left: The Miami Hurricanes would have done well to heed the warning on the sign. *(Jason J. Molyet/Newspaper Network of Central Ohio/Mansfield News Journal)*

Right: OSU fan Chad Karhoff of Glandorf, Ohio, came with his game face on for the Buckeyes' contest at Purdue. *(Kevin Graff/Newspaper Network of Central Ohio/Newark Advocate)*

Right: A fan snaps a picture of Brutus Buckeye during OSU's home win vs. Minnesota. *(Dante Smith/ Newspaper Network of Central Ohio/ Zanesville Times Recorder)*

Far right: Ohio State fans can't bring down the goalposts after Ohio State beat Michigan. *(Jason J. Molyet/Newspaper Network of Central Ohio/Mansfield News Journal)*

Opposite page: Ardent Buckeye fans get excited over first-half action at the Fiesta Bowl. *(Jason J. Molyet/Newspaper Network of Central Ohio/ Mansfield News Journal)*

Left: Tostitos chips fly around a fan with a makeshift sign celebrating the Fiesta Bowl win. *(Jason J. Molyet/Newspaper Network of Central Ohio/ Mansfield News Journal)*

Right: Based on the number of Ohio State backers at the Fiesta Bowl, this fan's sign certainly is correct. *(Jason J. Molyet/Newspaper Network of Central Ohio/Mansfield News Journal)*

Below: Jenny Williams of Dayton helps paint fellow Buckeye fan Dain Howell of Phoenix before the Fiesta Bowl. *(Dante Smith/ Newspaper Network of Central Ohio/Zanesville Times Recorder)*

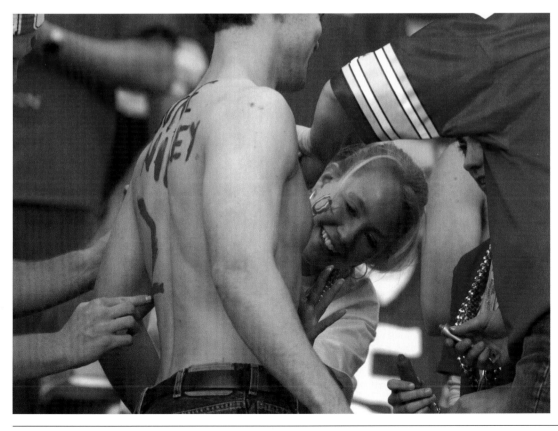

Above: T.J. Barnell, an OSU sophomore from Ironton, tries to keep freshman Taylor Waldo's ears warm before the Buckeyes' game vs. Purdue in West Lafayette, Ind. *(Kevin Graff/Newspaper Network of Central Ohio/Newark Advocate)*

Below: Buckeye fans hold up newspapers celebrating the Fiesta Bowl win. *(Jason J. Molyet/Newspaper Network of Central Ohio/Mansfield News Journal)*

Above: Jubilant OSU fans congratulate the Buckeyes after winning in overtime at Illinois. *(James Miller/Newspaper Network of Central Ohio/Marion Star)*

Right: A Buckeye fan prays during the first overtime in the Fiesta Bowl. *(Dante Smith/Newspaper Network of Central Ohio/Zanesville Times Recorder)*

Above: A Buckeye fan forms an "O" before Ohio State's game vs. San Jose State. *(Dante Smith/ Newspaper Network of Central Ohio/ Zanesville Times Recorder)*

Left: Maurice Clarett celebrates with fans after Ohio State defeated Michigan. *(Dave Polcyn/Newspaper Network of Central Ohio/Mansfield News Journal)*

Far left: Four-year-old Matthew Cubbison follows his father's lead and removes his hat for the playing of the national anthem prior to Ohio State's win over Texas Tech. *(Dante Smith/Newspaper Network of Central Ohio/Zanesville Times Recorder)*

Left: Ohio State fan Brian Sullivan cheers on the Buckeyes to victory over Michigan. *(Dante Smith/Newspaper Network of Central Ohio/Zanesville Times Recorder)*

Right: OSU fans chant O-H-I-O at the Fiesta Bowl. *(Jason J. Molyet/Newspaper Network of Central Ohio/Mansfield News Journal)*

Below: Buckeye fans celebrate Maurice Hall's winning touchdown vs. Michigan. *(Dave Polcyn/Newspaper Network of Central Ohio/Mansfield News Journal)*

OSU caps off dream season with chilly celebration

By Jon Spencer
Newspaper Network of Central Ohio

COLUMBUS — Getting to Miami quarterback Ken Dorsey on the final play of the Fiesta Bowl was much easier for Ohio State linebacker Cie Grant than performing his solo rendition of "Carmen Ohio."

Grant wasn't worried about forgetting the words to the alma mater. He was worried about his vocal chords freezing in mid-stanza.

"I was nervous and cold, and I was just getting over some illness," Grant said, "but once the emotion flowed, it was easy."

With Ohio Stadium turned into a block of ice, an announced crowd of 52,000 braved minus-three wind chill temperatures to attend a pep rally honoring the national champion Buckeyes.

It was a chance for Grant to show off his musical gifts and to see his pass-altering, title-clinching blitz of Dorsey appear larger than life as the team and its loyalists watched a highlight video of OSU's 14-0 season on the scoreboard's jumbo screen.

"I've seen that play quite a few times, and it didn't really hit me," said Grant, reflecting on the 31-24 double-overtime victory over Miami that gave

Ohio State its first consensus national championship since 1968.

"Seeing it on the jumbo, it really sunk in for the

Opposite page: OSU tight end Ben Hartsock preserves the moment for posterity. *(Jason J. Molyet/ Newspaper Network of Central Ohio/ Mansfield News Journal)*

Left: Players surround Buckeye linebacker Cie Grant after he sang "Carmen Ohio." *(Jason J. Molyet/Newspaper Network of Central Ohio/Mansfield News Journal)*

first time that we are national champions. It's amazing what this group has done ... it's a beautiful thing."

During the ceremony, Columbus Mayor Michael Coleman announced that part of Lane Avenue, which runs along the north side of campus, will be renamed "Champions Lane" as he unveiled the new street sign.

Gov. Bob Taft held up a No. 1 Ohio State jersey he plans to give Florida counterpart Jeb Bush next month in Washington, D.C., at a conference attended by the nation's governors.

The ceremony ended with Grant and the other seniors, including co-captains Mike Doss and Donnie Nickey, dotting the "i" as the Ohio State marching band performed its legendary Script Ohio.

All-America punter Andy Groom choked back tears as the seniors addressed the media afterwards.

"I looked up in the stands to see my parents for one last time and my dad was losing it," Groom said. "I never saw him cry in my life. It's hard to say bye."

Nickey doesn't plan to, at least when it comes to this senior class.

Opposite page: The Buckeyes get ready to come on to the field. *(Jason J. Molyet/Newspaper Network of Central Ohio/Mansfield News Journal)*

Left: Buckeye fans cheer as the team enters the stadium. *(Jason J. Molyet/ Newspaper Network of Central Ohio/ Mansfield News Journal)*

"We've connected on a family level," he said. "I have a lot of friends, but to go through what we've gone through (as a football team), there's a lot of love. We'll always love each other."

He also embraced the crowd, which came out on one of the coldest days in recent memory.

"To see all those people ... this is the last page in our book," Nickey said. "It's over for us. We went out on the highest of highs."

Coach Jim Tressel, who won four Division I-AA national championships at Youngstown State, was asked if dethroning Miami and snapping the Hurricanes' 34-game winning streak was the pinnacle of his career.

"Isn't pinnacle the single moment where you'll never be up that high again?" he said. "I hope not."

Fans who showed up at the event expecting to see Tressel's hair in cornrows were disappointed. He said in a preseason promise he would braid his hair that way if the Buckeyes finished the season

Left: Ohio State seniors dot the "i" in Script Ohio. *(William P. Cannon/Newspaper Network of Central Ohio/Lancaster Eagle-Gazette)*

unbeaten.

"I'm going to spring it on you when you least expect it," Tressel joked.

Doss was all smiles, too, as he talked about adjusting his diet.

"I kept eating Tostitos since last January," he said, poking fun at the sponsor of the Fiesta Bowl. "I finally don't have to eat them anymore."

Above: An optimistic fan proves it's never too early to look ahead. Next year's national championship game is at the Sugar Bowl. *(Jason J. Molyet/ Newspaper Network of Central Ohio/Mansfield News Journal)*

Above, left: Columbus Mayor Michael Coleman announces part of Lane Avenue will be renamed Champions Lane. *(William P. Cannon/Newspaper Network of Central Ohio/Lancaster Eagle-Gazette)*

Left: Bryce Gattshall, 10, of Grove City, Ohio, gets his poster signed by Will Smith and Maurice Clarett. *(William P. Cannon/ Newspaper Network of Central Ohio/Lancaster Eagle-Gazette)*

Commentary:
Closeness of team was key to success

By Jason Maddux
Newspaper Network of Central Ohio

COLUMBUS — In all the words written about the 2002 Ohio State national championship team, one fact is easy to overlook.

These guys seemed to really like each other.

Don't underestimate how much the camaraderie and respect for the team leaders played in the successful season.

Below: OSU safety Mike Doss congratulates coach Jim Tressel. *(Jason J. Molyet/Newspaper Network of Central Ohio/Mansfield News Journal)*

With so many college football teams so close talent-wise, it's often the other factors that make the difference.

Nine of the 13 departing seniors who met with the media after the celebration at the Horseshoe made the feelings for their classmates clear.

"With the things we've been through, we're connected on a family level," safety Donnie Nickey said. "We'll always love each other."

It was the small, behind-the-scene things that made the team closer.

"All you saw was the final product," three-time All American safety Mike Doss said. "You guys don't see the locker room, the training tables, the spring practice, all those things that make us a family."

Those bonding experiences even extended to the showers.

"I'll miss you guys getting me in the shower and throwing cold water on me," punter Andy Groom joked.

"All these guys from different situations and different walks of life ... this is where we wanted to be," said little-used cornerback Chris Conwell. "I'm just thankful. I love you guys."

They will be linked forever, and it seems they've already given that some thought.

Nickey and Doss said they plan to write a book about the season. At first it seemed they were joking, but who knows?

The Doss legend will continue to grow. Ohio State has had few better leaders than No. 2. Everyone knows the story about how he returned to Ohio State to win a national championship ... making his decision to stay as he was addressing the media.

And he was successful, even being as superstitious as to eat Tostitos chips during the season because they sponsored the national championship game in the Fiesta Bowl.

Doss even led the team in dotting the "i" in Script Ohio at the national title celebration, trying his best to strut out like the sousaphone player does.

He and coach Jim Tressel seem a perfect pair — both about family and working hard with a healthy slice of religion thrown in.

Speaking of Tressel ... you can't say enough about how he molded this team into the family the seniors described. Most of the key players weren't his recruits. But he shaped this team in his image and made them winners.

I wonder how Tressel celebrated. He just doesn't seem the celebrating type. Even after the celebration, while most coaches would have been happy to sit back, he was making sure there were enough chairs for all the seniors to sit in during the media interviews. When there weren't, he stole some from the rows lined up for the media and set them up for this players.

No detail is too small.

So how do you replace those guys, coach?

"It's a great challenge for the upcoming seniors," he said, understating the obvious.

Tressel said it's "not just a football challenge" next year,

meaning the Buckeyes will have to recapture some of the magic the senior leaders provided.

The players had each other's backs, as little-used senior fullback Jack Tucker said. They had faith in each other.

There's no doubt this team had great talent. But did it have more than Archie Griffin's teams of the mid-1970s? Or the Hoying-George-Glenn teams of the mid-1990s? Probably not.

When you look back on such a fragile season, the bottom line is this team won 14 games. So they had something more than those other teams. Call it chemistry, leadership, luck or the X factor. It was there.

"You guys are the best friends I've had in my life," Groom said.

That type of chemistry, confidence and love doesn't occur by accident — or very often. And you can't practice it or force it. It just happens.

So how do you get it back when players leave?

Tressel will recruit the kind of young men he feels will continue what was started this year. He will do it his way, which means that a sense of family, values and purpose will reign.

Those are winning traits. Just ask the 2002 Buckeyes.

Left: Coach Jim Tressel addresses the crowd in front of the national championship trophy.
(William P. Cannon/Newspaper Network of Central Ohio/Lancaster Eagle-Gazette)

Below: Ohio State punter Andy Groom can't control his emotions during the celebration ceremony. When he looked into the stands, he saw his father crying. He had never seen him cry before.
(Jason J. Molyet/Newspaper Network of Central Ohio/Mansfield News Journal)

2002 Ohio State University Buckeyes Roster

No.	Name	Pos.	Ht.	Wg.	Cl.	Elg.	Hometown/High School or J.C.
49	John Adams	FB	5-11	220	Jr.	So.	Springfield, Ohio/Northeastern
10	Tucker Allen	LB	5-11	220	So.	Fr.	Columbus, Ohio/Upper Arlington
26	Will Allen **	FS	6-2	190	Jr.	Jr.	Dayton, Ohio/Wayne
54	Tim Anderson **	DT	6-4	289	Jr.	Jr.	Clyde, Ohio/Clyde
96	David Andrews	TE	6-2	225	Jr.	So.	Bloomingburg, Ohio/Miami Trace
60	Kyle Andrews	LS	5-11	245	Jr.	So.	Middletown, Ohio/Middletown
83	Redgie Arden	TE	6-4	240	So.	Fr.	Ironton, Ohio/Ironton
78	Bryce Bishop *	OG	6-3	312	Sr.	Jr.	Miami, Fla./Killian
51	Mike Bogart	OG	6-3	290	Jr.	Jr.	Cleveland, Ohio/St. Ignatius
91	Jason Bond **	LB	6-3	240	Sr.	Jr.	Worthington, Ohio/Watterson
19	LeAndre Boone	FS	6-1	215	So.	Fr.	Portsmouth, Va./Herndon
58	Joe Bradley	LB	6-3	213	So.	Fr.	Upper Arlington, Ohio/Upper Arlington
1	Bobby Britton **	CB	5-11	194	Jr.	Jr.	Jacksonville, Fla./Raines
87	Jason Caldwell	TE	6-5	265	Jr.	So.	Mentor, Ohio/Mentor
42	Bobby Carpenter	LB	6-3	240	Fr.	Fr.	Lancaster, Ohio/Lancaster
8	Drew Carter *	SE	6-4	200	Sr.	Jr.	Solon, Ohio/Solon
14	Angelo Chattams *	FL	5-11	185	So.	So.	Dayton, Ohio/Chaminade-Julienne
3	Bam Childress *	FL	5-10	185	Jr.	So.	Warrensville Heights, Ohio/Chanel
13	Maurice Clarett	TB	6-0	230	Fr.	Fr.	Youngstown, Ohio/Harding
63	Adrien Clarke **	OG	6-5	355	Sr.	Jr.	Shaker Heights, Ohio/Shaker Heights
81	R.J. Coleman	TE	6-5	265	Fr.	Fr.	Clarksburg, W.Va./Byrd
59	John Conroy	OL	6-3	275	So.	Fr.	Bay Village, Ohio/St. Ignatius
20	Chris Conwell	CB	5-10	190	5th	Sr.	Shaker Heights, Ohio/Shaker Heights
79	Ryan Cook	OT	6-7	305	So.	Fr.	Martinsville, Ind./Martinsville
74	Bryce Culver	DE	6-4	225	Jr.	So.	Lewis Center, Ohio/Olentangy
5	Mike D'Andrea	LB	6-3	240	Fr.	Fr.	Avon Lake, Ohio/Avon Lake
66	Doug Datish	OT	6-5	290	Fr.	Fr.	Warren, Ohio/Howland
36	Michael DeMaria	TB	5-9	190	Jr.	So.	Oregon, Ohio/Cardinal Stritch
2	Mike Doss ***	SS	5-11	204	Sr.	Sr.	Canton, Ohio/McKinley
53	Ivan Douglas *	OT	6-8	305	Sr.	Jr.	University Heights, Ohio/Benedictine
72	T.J. Downing	OL	6-5	280	Fr.	Fr.	Canton, Ohio/GlenOak
33	Tyler Everett	DB	6-1	185	Fr.	Fr.	Canton, Ohio/McKinley
37	Dustin Fox *	CB	6-0	190	So.	So.	Canton, Ohio/GlenOak
75	Simon Fraser *	DE	6-6	250	So.	So.	Upper Arlington, Ohio/Upper Arlington
7	Chris Gamble *	SE	6-2	180	So.	So.	Sunrise, Fla./Dillard
65	Steve Graef	DE	6-2	240	Jr.	So.	Uniontown, Ohio/Lake
6	Cie Grant ***	LB	6-1	220	5th	Sr.	New Philadelphia, Ohio/New Philadelphia
94	Marcus Green	DT	6-3	300	So.	So.	Louisville, Ky./Male
18	Andy Groom **	P/H	6-1	185	5th	Sr.	Columbus, Ohio/Bishop Hartley
28	Maurice Hall *	TB	5-10	200	So.	So.	Columbus, Ohio/Brookhaven
82	Roy Hall	WR	6-3	228	Fr.	Fr.	Lyndhurst, Ohio/Brush
80	Ryan Hamby	TE	6-5	240	So.	Fr.	Cincinnati, Ohio/Moeller
4	Rob Harley	DB	6-2	202	So.	So.	Elmhurst, Ill./York
88	Ben Hartsock **	TE	6-4	264	Sr.	Jr.	Chillicothe, Ohio/Unioto
47	A.J. Hawk	LB	6-2	230	Fr.	Fr.	Centerville, Ohio/Centerville
84	John Hollins	SE	6-2	205	Jr.	So.	Huber Heights, Ohio/Wayne
17	Santonio Holmes	WR	5-11	170	Fr.	Fr.	Belle Glade, Fla./Glades Central
81	Andre Hooks	WR	6-2	205	Jr.	So.	Canton, Ohio/Canton McKinley
23	Josh Huston *	P-K	6-1	195	Jr.	So.	Findlay, Ohio/Findlay
13	Harlen Jacobs *	CB	6-1	197	Jr.	So.	Atlanta, Ga./Douglass
12	Michael Jenkins **	SE	6-5	215	Jr.	Jr.	Tampa, Fla./Leto
38	Branden Joe *	FB	6-0	245	Jr.	So.	Westerville, Ohio/South
52	Mike Kne	OT	6-4	300	Jr.	Jr.	Cleveland, Ohio/St. Ignatius
17	Craig Kolk	WR	6-1	192	Fr.	Fr.	Wayne, N.J./Wayne Valley
16	Craig Krenzel **	QB	6-4	225	Sr.	Jr.	Utica, Mich./Henry Ford II
57	Mike Kudla	DE	6-3	255	Fr.	Fr.	Medina, Ohio/Highland
70	Scott Kuhnhein *	OG	6-4	285	5th	Sr.	Fort Thomas, Ky./Highlands
86	Maurice Lee	FL	5-10	180	Sr.	Jr.	Cleveland, Ohio/South
37	Jamal Luke	WR	5-11	175	Sr.	Jr.	Columbus, Ohio/Tifffin University
55	Nick Mangold	OL	6-4	270	Fr.	Fr.	Kettering, Ohio/Alter
41	Thomas Matthews	SS	6-2	210	Jr.	So.	Ft. Lauderdale, Fla./Dillard
62	John McLaughlin	OT	6-6	290	Jr.	So.	Fairview Park, Ohio/St. Ignatius
15	Scott McMullen **	QB	6-3	215	Sr.	Jr.	Granville, Ohio/Granville
11	Richard McNutt **	CB	5-11	178	Sr.	Jr.	Park Forest, Ill./Rich East
62	Jeremy Miller	LS	6-0	200	Sr.	Jr.	Lewistown, Ohio/Indian Lake
32	Brandon Mitchell	DB	6-3	190	Fr.	Fr.	Atlanta, Ga./Mays
3	Steven Moore	CB	5-10	185	Jr.	So.	Columbus, Ohio/St. Charles
61	Ben Nash	OL	6-3	275	So.	Fr.	Westerville, Ohio/Westerville
25	Donnie Nickey ***	FS	6-3	203	5th	Sr.	Plain City, Ohio/Jonathan Alder
85	Mike Nugent *	PK	5-10	170	So.	So.	Centerville, Ohio/Centerville
64	Adam Olds	OG	6-4	290	So.	Fr.	Dublin, Ohio/Dublin Coffman
71	Shane Olivea **	OT	6-5	310	Jr.	Jr.	Cedarhurst, N.Y./Lawrence
36	Pat O'Neill **	LB	6-3	230	Sr.	Jr.	Cuyahoga Falls, Ohio/Walsh Jesuit
18	Jim Otis	QB	5-10	200	Jr.	So.	Chesterfield, Mo./Christian Brothers CLG
46	Fred Pagac Jr. **	LB	6-1	225	Sr.	Jr.	Dublin, Ohio/Dublin Coffman
20	Roshawn Parker	RB	5-11	219	Jr.	So.	Columbus, Ohio/Eastmoor
42	Steve Pavelka	RB	5-7	165	So.	So.	Springfield, Ohio/Shawnee
98	Joel Penton	DE	6-5	255	Fr.	Fr.	Van Wert, Ohio/Van Wert
97	Kenny Peterson **	DT	6-4	290	5th	Sr.	Canton, Ohio/McKinley
23	Scott Petroff	WR	5-11	180	Sr.	Jr.	Winter Park, Fla./Lake Howell
90	Quinn Pitcock	DL	6-4	285	Fr.	Fr.	Piqua, Ohio/Piqua
44	Robert Reynolds **	LB	6-3	234	Jr.	Jr.	Bowling Green, Ky./Bowling Green
99	Jay Richardson	DE	6-5	245	Fr.	Fr.	Dublin, Ohio/Scioto
34	JaJa Riley	TB	6-2	205	So.	Fr.	San Diego, Calif./Mission Bay
24	Mike Roberts	CB	5-11	178	Fr.	Fr.	Toronto, Canada/Central Technical
30	Lydell Ross *	TB	6-0	210	So.	So	Tampa, Fla./Gaither
19	Matt Russell	K	5-11	184	Sr.	Sr.	Napoleon, Ohio/Napoleon
21	Nate Salley	DB	6-3	180	Fr.	Fr.	Fort Lauderdale, Fla./St. Thomas Aquinas
21	B.J. Sander *	P	6-3	212	Sr.	Jr.	Cincinnati, Ohio/Roger Bacon
92	Tim Schafer	DE	6-5	250	Fr.	Fr.	Upper Arlington, Ohio/Upper Arlington
43	Brandon Schnittker	FB	6-1	250	So.	Fr.	Sandusky, Ohio/Perkins
56	Darrion Scott **	DE	6-3	271	Jr.	Jr.	Charleston, W. Va./Capital
77	Rob Sims	OL	6-4	290	Fr.	Fr.	Macedonia, Ohio/Nordonia
14	Antonio Smith	DB	5-10	175	Fr.	Fr.	Columbus, Ohio/Beechcroft
10	Troy Smith	QB	6-1	205	Fr.	Fr.	Glenville, Ohio/Glenville
93	Will Smith **	DE	6-4	250	Jr.	Jr.	Utica, N.Y./Proctor
50	Michael Stafford	OT	6-3	280	5th	Sr.	Upper Arlington, Ohio/Upper Arlington
76	Alex Stepanovich **	C	6-4	310	Jr.	Jr.	Berea, Ohio/Berea
95	David Thompson *	DT	6-5	290	5th	Sr.	Paterson, N.J./Eastside
24	Matt Trombitas	QB	6-5	224	So.	Fr.	Dublin, Ohio/Dublin Coffman
48	Jack Tucker	FB	6-2	235	5th	Sr.	Cypress, Calif./Cerritos C.C.
86	Kyle Turano	P/K	6-0	195	Jr.	Jr.	Worthington, Ohio/Kilbourne
69	Andree Tyree	C	6-3	280	So.	Fr.	London, Ohio/London
5	Jeremy Uhlenhake	K	5-11	200	5th	Sr.	Celina, Ohio/Celina
49	E.J. Underwood	DB	6-1	175	Fr.	Fr.	Hamilton, Ohio/Hamilton
4	Chris Vance *	FL	6-2	180	Sr.	Sr.	Fort Myers, Fla./Fort Scott C.C.
9	Bryan Weaver	P/DB	5-10	196	So.	So.	Sunbury, Ohio/Big Walnut
89	Stan White Jr.	LB	6-3	230	Fr.	Fr.	Baltimore, Md./Gilman School
67	Kurt Wilhelm	LS	6-0	230	Jr.	So.	Lorain, Ohio/Elyria Catholic
35	Matt Wilhelm ***	LB	6-5	245	Sr.	Sr.	Lorain, Ohio/Elyria Catholic
52	Sam Williams	DL	6-3	237	So.	So.	Middletown, Md./Middletown
73	Steve Winner	OL	6-6	270	So.	Fr.	Dublin, Ohio/Dublin Coffman
11	Mike Young	WR	6-5	205	Sr.	Jr.	Middletown, Ohio/Middletown
9	Justin Zwick	QB	6-4	210	Fr.	Fr.	Massillon, Ohio/Washington

*Indicates no. of varsity letters earned

Buckeyes Season Statistics

TEAM STATISTICS:

	OSU	OPP
SCORING	410	183
Points Per Game	29.3	13.1
FIRST DOWNS	245	243
Rushing	133	72
Passing	106	155
Penalty	6	16
RUSHING YARDAGE	2,678	1,088
Yards gained rushing	3,000	1,481
Yards lost rushing	322	393
Rushing Attempts	629	418
Average Per Rush	4.3	2.6
Average Per Game	191.3	77.7
TDs Rushing	31	5
PASSING YARDAGE	2,425	3,404
Att-Comp-Int	280-173-7	546-315-18
Average Per Pass	8.7	6.2
Average Per Catch	14.0	10.8
Average Per Game	173.2	243.1
TDs Passing	14	14
TOTAL OFFENSE	5,103	4,492
Total Plays	909	964
Average Per Play	5.6	4.7
Average Per Game	364.5	320.9
KICK RETURNS: #-YARDS	37-747	33-711
PUNT RETURNS: #-YARDS	43-358	33-423
INT RETURNS: #-YARDS	18-199	7-87
KICK RETURN AVERAGE	20.2	21.5
PUNT RETURN AVERAGE	8.3	12.8
INT RETURN AVERAGE	11.1	12.4
FUMBLES-LOST	17-10	20-12
PENALTIES-YARDS	76-571	66-561
Average Per Game	40.8	40.1
PUNTS-YARDS	61-2,697	76-2,821
Average Per Punt	44.2	37.1
Net punt average	37.3	32.4
TIME OF POSSESSION/GAME	31:43	28:17
3RD-DOWN CONVERSIONS	64/179	78/219
3rd-Down Pct.	36%	36%
4TH-DOWN CONVERSIONS	12/18	11/27
4th-Down Pct.	67%	41%
SACKS BY-YARDS	40-227	32-167
MISC YARDS	24	58
TOUCHDOWNS SCORED	48	19
FIELD GOALS-ATTEMPTS	25-28	17-25
PAT-ATTEMPTS	45-46	16-17
ATTENDANCE	827,904	313,597
Games/Avg Per Game	8/103,488	5/62,719

SCORE BY QUARTERS	1st	2nd	3rd	4th	OT	Total
Ohio State	75	112	120	82	21	410
Opponents	59	53	31	33	7	183

INDIVIDUAL STATISTICS:

RUSHING	GP	Att	Gain	Loss	Net	Avg	TD	Long	Avg/G
Clarett, Maurice	11	222	1266	29	1237	5.6	16	59	112.5
Ross, Lydell	14	166	648	29	619	3.7	6	36	44.2
Hall, Maurice	14	78	396	26	370	4.7	4	28	26.4
Krenzel, Craig	14	125	548	180	368	2.9	3	29	26.3
Gamble, Chris	14	3	49	0	49	16.3	1	43	3.5
Riley, JaJa	6	12	47	3	44	3.7	0	10	7.3
Nickey, Donnie	14	1	28	0	28	28.0	0	28	2.0
Parker, Roshawn	1	1	6	0	6	6.0	0	6	6.0
Otis, Jim	1	1	2	0	2	2.0	0	2	2.0
McMullen, Scott	5	4	8	7	1	0.2	1	7	0.2
Schnittker, Brandon	14	1	1	0	1	1.0	0	1	0.1
Joe, Branden	12	1	1	0	1	1.0	0	1	0.1
Groom, Andy	14	2	0	16	-16	-8.0	0	0	-1.1
TEAM	11	12	0	32	-32	-2.7	0	0	-2.9
Total	14	629	3000	322	2678	4.3	31	59	191.3
Opponents	14	418	1481	393	1088	2.6	5	46	77.7

PASSING	GP	Effic	Att-Cmp-Int	Pct	Yds	TD	Lng	Avg/G
Krenzel, Craig	14	140.90	249-148-7	59.4	2110	12	57	150.7
McMullen, Scott	5	187.29	31-25-0	80.6	315	2	28	63.0
Total	14	146.04	280-173-7	61.8	2425	14	57	173.2
Opponents	14	111.93	546-315-18	57.7	3404	14	58	243.1

RECEIVING	GP	No.	Yds	Avg	TD	Long	Avg/G
Jenkins, Michael	14	61	1076	17.6	6	50	76.9
Gamble, Chris	14	31	499	16.1	0	57	35.6
Hartsock, Ben	14	17	137	8.1	2	20	9.8
Vance, Chris	11	13	178	13.7	3	37	16.2
Clarett, Maurice	11	12	104	8.7	2	26	9.5
Carter, Drew	11	10	147	14.7	0	28	13.4
Ross, Lydell	14	10	75	7.5	0	28	5.4
Hall, Maurice	14	5	43	8.6	0	16	3.1
Arden, Redgie	11	4	50	12.5	0	19	4.5
Childress, Bam	12	4	47	11.8	0	17	3.9
Hamby, Ryan	13	2	29	14.5	1	18	2.2
Schnittker, Brandon	14	2	27	13.5	0	15	1.9
Hollins, John	5	1	14	14.0	0	14	2.8
McMullen, Scott	5	1	-1	-1.0	0	0	-0.2
Total	14	173	2425	14.0	14	57	173.2
Opponents	14	315	3404	10.8	14	58	243.1

PUNT RETURNS	No.	Yds	Avg	TD	Long
Gamble, Chris	35	293	8.4	0	27
Doss, Mike	4	25	6.2	0	14
Nickey, Donnie	1	14	14.0	0	0
Vance, Chris	1	5	5.0	0	5
Fox, Dustin	1	10	10.0	0	0
Jenkins, Michael	1	11	11.0	0	0
Total	43	358	8.3	0	27
Opponents	33	423	12.8	0	52

INDIVIDUAL STATISTICS (cont):

INTERCEPTIONS	No.	Yds	Avg	TD	Long
Gamble, Chris	4	40	10.0	1	40
Fox, Dustin	3	12	4.0	0	12
Wilhelm, Matt	2	0	0.0	0	0
Allen, Will	2	0	0.0	0	0
Hawk, A.J.	2	44	22.0	1	34
Doss, Mike	2	80	40.0	1	45
Everett, Tyler	1	0	0.0	0	0
Grant, Cie	1	23	23.0	0	23
Smith, Will	1	0	0.0	0	0
Total	18	199	11.1	3	45
Opponents	7	87	12.4	0	28

KICK RETURNS	No.	Yds	Avg	TD	Long
Hall, Maurice	19	434	22.8	0	45
Gamble, Chris	11	253	23.0	0	56
Joe, Brandon	2	10	5.0	0	10
Doss, Mike	2	37	18.5	0	24
Schnittker, Brandon	1	11	11.0	0	11
Tucker, Jack	1	0	0.0	0	0
Vance, Chris	1	2	2.0	0	2
Total	37	747	20.2	0	56
Opponents	33	711	21.5	0	67

FUMBLE RETURNS	No.	Yds	Avg	TD	Long
Nickey, Donnie	1	7	7.0	0	7
Kudla, Mike	1	17	17.0	0	17
Total	2	24	12.0	0	17
Opponents	1	58	58.0	0	58

FIELD GOALS	FGM-FGA	Pct	01-19	20-29	30-39	40-49	50-99	Lg	Blk
Nugent, Mike	25-28	89.3	0-0	6-6	9-10	9-11	1-1	51	0

TOTAL OFFENSE	G	Plays	Rush	Pass	Total	Avg/G
Krenzel, Craig	14	374	368	2110	2478	177.0
Clarett, Maurice	11	222	1237	0	1237	112.5
Ross, Lydell	14	166	619	0	619	44.2
Hall, Maurice	14	78	370	0	370	26.4
McMullen, Scott	5	35	1	315	316	63.2
Gamble, Chris	14	3	49	0	49	3.5
Riley, JaJa	6	12	44	0	44	7.3
Nickey, Donnie	14	1	28	0	28	2.0
Parker, Roshawn	1	1	6	0	6	6.0
Otis, Jim	1	1	2	0	2	2.0
Schnittker, Brandon	14	1	1	0	1	0.1
Joe, Branden	12	1	1	0	1	0.1
Groom, Andy	14	2	-16	0	-16	-1.1
TEAM	11	12	-32	0	-32	-2.9
Total	14	909	2678	2425	5103	364.5
Opponents	14	964	1088	3404	4492	320.9

OVERALL INDIVIDUAL DEFENSIVE STATISTICS:

DEFENSIVE LEADERS	GP	Solo	Ast	Total	TFL/Yds	No-Yds	Int-Yds	BrUp	QBH	Rcv-Yds	FF	Kick	Saf
Wilhelm, Matt	14	79	42	121	19.5-49	3.0-15	2-0	3	.	.	2	.	.
Doss, Mike	14	65	42	107	5.0-7	.	2-80	8	.	1-0	.	.	.
Fox, Dustin	14	67	17	84	2.5-4	.	3-12	14	.	1-0	3	1	.
Grant, Cie	13	50	21	71	10.0-47	4.0-36	1-23	.	.	.	.	.	.
Nickey, Donnie	14	44	23	67	1.0-2	.	.	2	.	2-7	.	2	.
Reynolds, Robert	13	39	23	62	3.5-16	1.0-4	.	.	.	.	1	.	.
Smith, Will	14	41	18	59	12.5-42	5.5-31	1-0	4	.	1-0	.	1	.
Peterson, Kenny	14	26	17	43	9.5-40	6.0-31	.	6	.	.	2	.	.
Scott, Darrion	13	22	21	43	9.5-44	8.5-42	.	4	.	2-0	3	.	.
Thompson, David	14	23	19	42	7.5-28	4.5-24	.	2	.	1-0	.	.	.
Anderson, Tim	12	16	20	36	2.5-10	2.5-9	.	3	1	1-0	.	.	.
Allen, Will	13	22	10	32	2.5-25	1.0-11	2-0	.	.	1-0	.	.	.
Hawk, A.J.	14	13	13	26	3.5-16	0.5-5	2-44	.	.	.	.	.	.
Gamble, Chris	14	21	3	24	1.0-2	.	4-40	6	.	.	.	.	.
Underwood, E.J.	14	17	4	21	.	.	.	3	.	.	.	.	.
Fraser, Simon	14	13	7	20	7.0-32	5.0-19	.	5	.	.	2	.	.
McNutt, Richard	6	10	6	16	.	.	.	.	.	.	.	.	.
Carpenter, Bobby	8	4	12	.	.	.	.	.	.	.	.	.	.
Kudla, Mike	14	5	7	12	1.0-2	.	.	.	.	1-17	.	.	.
Pagac, Fred	9	8	3	11	2.0-2	.	.	.	.	.	.	.	.
Everett, Tyler	9	7	4	11	.	.	1-0	.	.	.	.	.	.
Conwell, Chris	14	7	1	8	.	.	.	.	.	.	.	.	.
D'Andrea, Mike	12	4	3	7	.	.	.	.	.	.	1	.	.
Britton, Bobby	10	3	4	7	.	.	.	2	.	.	.	.	.
Salley, Nate	14	3	3	6	.	.	.	.	.	.	.	.	.
Jacobs, Harlen	6	6	.	6	.	.	.	.	1	.	.	.	.
Bond, Jason	13	2	2	4	.	.	.	.	.	.	.	.	.
TEAM	11	1	2	3	.	.	.	.	.	.	.	.	1
Moore, Steven	9	3	.	3	.	.	.	.	.	.	.	.	.
Childress, Bam	12	2	1	3	.	.	.	1	.	.	.	.	.
O'Neill, Pat	12	2	.	2	.	.	.	.	.	.	.	.	.
Tucker, Jack	11	1	1	2	.	.	.	.	.	.	.	.	.
Groom, Andy	14	1	1	2	.	.	.	.	.	.	.	.	.
Green, Marcus	10	1	1	2	.	.	.	.	.	.	.	.	.
Andrews, Kyle	14	1	.	1	.	.	.	.	.	.	.	.	.
Nugent, Mike	14	1	.	1	.	.	.	.	.	.	.	.	.
Stead, Nate	6	1	.	1	.	.	.	.	.	.	.	.	.
Schnittker, Brandon	14	1	.	1	.	.	.	.	.	.	.	.	.
Arden, Redgie	11	.	1	1	.	.	.	.	.	.	.	.	.
Andrews, David	3	1	.	1	.	.	.	.	.	.	.	.	.
Krenzel, Craig	14	1	.	1	.	.	.	.	.	.	.	.	.
Clarett, Maurice	11	1	.	1	.	.	.	.	.	1-0	1	.	.
Jenkins, Michael	14	.	.	.	.	.	.	.	.	.	.	1	.
Total	14	639	344	983	100-368	40-227	18-199	68	1	12-24	17	4	1
Opponents	14	611	434	1045	85-285	32-167	7-87	28	6	10-58	11	1	.

Has it sunk in yet?

Has it sunk in yet?

This was the most popular question asked of nearly every Ohio State football player after clinching the national championship at the Fiesta Bowl on Jan. 3.

Players weren't the only ones waiting for reality to hit. In my nine years covering the Buckeye football team, never have I been left with such a "Did that just happen?" feeling as I was in the minutes, hours and even days after the game.

Dave Maetzold

Whether you attended the game or saw it on television, the true reality of winning a national championship sinks in slowly. As the game is replayed over the years, as players in the game become immortalized as Buckeye legends, and as the championship banners fade and fray in the wind, the reality becomes as hard and true as concrete.

This dream season had its life flash before its eyes no less than five times; at Cincinnati, at Purdue, at Illinois, against Michigan and again in the Fiesta Bowl. I was fortunate enough to be on the field to witness firsthand the intangible qualities of teamwork, toughness and perseverance that pulled the Buckeyes through each time. That's how dreams become reality.

This won't be the last national championship season for the Buckeyes, but as I told my 15-year old son just before kickoff — "Remember this, you may never see anything like it again."

That's a reality I'll cherish forever.

Dave Maetzold is sports director of NBC 4 in Columbus.